THE SOCIETY OF ILLUSTRATORS
38TH ANNUAL OF AMERICAN ILLUSTRATION
ILLUSTRATORS 38

From the exhibition held in the galleries of the
Society of Illustrators Museum of American Illustration
128 East 63rd Street, New York City
February 10 - April 13, 1996

Society of Illustrators, Inc.
128 East 63rd Street, New York, NY 10021

ISBN 0-8230-6553-7
Library of Congress Catalog Card Number 59-10849

Published for the Society of Illustrators by:
Rotovision S.A.
7 rue du Bugnon
1299 Crans
Switzerland

Distributed to the trade in the United States
Watson-Guptill Publications
1515 Broadway, New York, NY 10036

Distributed throughout the rest of the world by:
Rotovision Sales Office
Sheridan House
112/116A Western Road
Hove BN3 1DD ENGLAND
Tel. +44 1273 727268
Fax. +44 1273 727269

Edited by Jill Bossert
Cover painting by Brad Holland
Cover design by Fred Woodward
Interior design by Doug Johnson and Ryuichi Minakawa
Layout and Typesetting by Naomi Minakawa

Printed in Singapore

Photo Credits: Rob Day by Sam Scott, Etienne Delessert by Marcel Imsand,
Eddie Guy by Marianne Barcellona, Arthur Hockstein by Dennis Chalkin, Mirko Ilic by Poul Hans Lange,
Gary Kelley by Murray Tinkelman, John Maggard by Wendt Worldwide Photography,
Gene Mydlowski by C. Saksa, Jerry Pinkney by John Lei

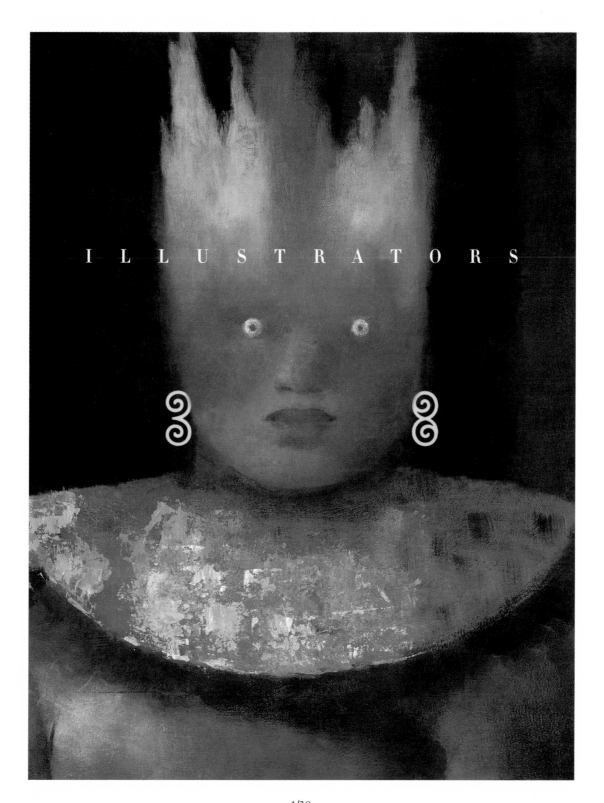

ILLUSTRATORS

Published by Rotovision S.A.

Portrait by Brad Holland

The Best—one wonders if there even is such a thing. As the field of illustration becomes progressively more competitive, it grows more difficult to make that determination. To be selected from over 6,000 submissions is quite an achievement, particularly in a market which has grown intolerant of mediocrity. If you work in this field, have worked for any length of time and done so successfully, you are clearly not cut from the common cloth. To do it at all, on demand and on time—time after time—is the real accomplishment.

The challenge for illustrators is not merely to get work into our annual show, but to create pictures with sufficient clarity and originality, with enough skill, to be asked to do it again. Our show is the tip of the iceberg of the many tens of thousands of artistic visions of genuine excellence produced by illustrators every year. The best is a relative term and a highly subjective one, too, as the standards of the industry surge upward and the "best" becomes better yet.

Illustrators 38 was a great exhibition, one of the best in recent memory, as these pages will certainly show. We are grateful to Chris Payne, its Chair, and Wendell Minor, the Assistant Chair— great artists who have also demonstrated a remarkable talent for organization, management, and diplomacy, that made this exhibition happen. Our thanks to the distinguished juries and the category Chairs who diligently labored to funnel the submissions down to a manageable size; to the Society staff for separating, grouping and presenting the materials for consideration; to the Past Chairmen's Committee for overseeing the process; and to the Publications Committee for producing the most handsome and revealing book in all the industry, year after year. Our heartiest congratulations to all of you with work in the show and to the award winners. For the thousands who pass through the doors of the Society of Illustrators Museum of American Illustration and marvel at what you've done, you have provided a vivid and telling mirror of our culture and our time. There is nothing quite so gratifying as seeing the light go on in the eyes of a young art student who then leaves the building with a new-found drive for excellence. You have much to take pride in.

Vincent DiFate
President
1995 - 1996

THE ILLUSTRATORS HALL OF FAME

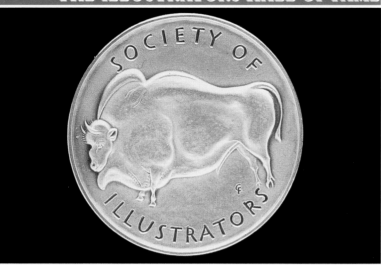

Since 1958, the Society of Illustrators has elected to its Hall of Fame artists recognized for their "distinguished achievement in the art of illustration." The list of previous winners is truly a "Who's Who" of illustration. Former Presidents of the Society meet annually to elect those who will be so honored.

HALL OF FAME COMMITTEE 1996

CHAIRMAN, **Murray Tinkelman**

CHAIRMAN EMERITUS, **Willis Pyle**

FORMER PRESIDENTS,

Diane Dillon, Peter Fiore, Charles McVicker, Wendell Minor, Howard Munce, Alvin J. Pimsler, Warren Rogers, Eileen Hedy Schultz, Shannon Stirnweis, David K. Stone, John Witt

HALL OF FAME LAUREATES 1996

Herb Tauss
Anton Otto Fischer*
Winsor McCay*
Violet Oakley*
Mead Schaeffer*

HALL OF FAME LAUREATES 1958-1995

Norman Rockwell 1958	John Clymer 1982
Dean Cornwell 1959	Henry P. Raleigh* 1982
Harold Von Schmidt 1959	Eric (Carl Erickson)* 1982
Fred Cooper 1960	Mark English 1983
Floyd Davis 1961	Noel Sickles* 1983
Edward Wilson 1962	Franklin Booth* 1983
Walter Biggs 1963	Neysa Moran McMein* 1984
Arthur William Brown 1964	John LaGatta* 1984
Al Parker 1965	James Williamson* 1984
Al Dorne 1966	Charles Marion Russell* 1985
Robert Fawcett 1967	Arthur Burdett Frost* 1985
Peter Helck 1968	Robert Weaver 1985
Austin Briggs 1969	Rockwell Kent* 1986
Rube Goldberg 1970	Al Hirschfeld 1986
Stevan Dohanos 1971	Haddon Sundblom* 1987
Ray Prohaska 1972	Maurice Sendak 1987
Jon Whitcomb 1973	René Bouché* 1988
Tom Lovell 1974	Pruett Carter* 1988
Charles Dana Gibson* 1974	Robert T. McCall 1988
N.C. Wyeth* 1974	Erté 1989
Bernie Fuchs 1975	John Held Jr.* 1989
Maxfield Parrish* 1975	Arthur Ignatius Keller* 1989
Howard Pyle* 1975	Burt Silverman 1990
John Falter 1976	Robert Riggs* 1990
Winslow Homer* 1976	Morton Roberts* 1990
Harvey Dunn* 1976	Donald Teague 1991
Robert Peak 1977	Jessie Willcox Smith* 1991
Wallace Morgan* 1977	William A. Smith* 1991
J.C. Leyendecker* 1977	Joe Bowler 1992
Coby Whitmore 1978	Edwin A. Georgi* 1992
Norman Price* 1978	Dorothy Hood* 1992
Frederic Remington* 1978	Robert McGinnis 1993
Ben Stahl 1979	Thomas Nast* 1993
Edwin Austin Abbey* 1979	Coles Phillips* 1993
Lorraine Fox* 1979	Harry Anderson 1994
Saul Tepper 1980	Elizabeth Shippen Green* 1994
Howard Chandler Christy* 1980	Ben Shahn* 1994
James Montgomery Flagg* 1980	James Avati 1995
Stan Galli 1981	McClelland Barclay* 1995
Frederic R. Gruger* 1981	Joseph Clement Coll* 1995
John Gannam* 1981	Frank E. Schoonover* 1995

*Presented posthumously

In the continuing process of recognizing unique talent and accomplishment by the Society of Illustrators Hall of Fame, one of its newest inductees, Herb Tauss, wonderfully extends this tradition.

The interesting trajectory of his career from his only formal training in high school to an eighteen-dollar-a-week apprenticeship at Traeger Phillips Studio running errands and cutting mattes, to his first illustration for *Pageant Magazine* for eighty-four dollars, to eventually joining the Charles E. Cooper Studio, was a long, expansive evolution.

There followed a life-changing opportunity of working for British women's magazines and extended European travel with his family. This was an enriching learning experience exceeding all expectations.

In sum, this maturing led to thirty years of drawings, paintings, and sculpture for major national magazines and many books, including a host of paperback book covers. His works are included in private and governmental collections. He is the recipient of further recognition by the Society of Illustrators as a frequent medal winner.

A self-confessed perfectionist, he says, "To be a good artist is difficult. You must be emotionally involved with what you're doing." As fellow illustrator Murray Tinkelman has said, "He has constantly re-invented himself over the decades. Evolving on every level, both stylistically and thematically, his work is remarkable for its consistent foundation of emotional honesty and sincerity."

Today, new modes and concepts are proliferating and markets are rapidly changing in a pluralistic, unstable world. Herb is a beacon of the continuing powers of traditional painting and drawing enlivened by deep love and belief in the concept.

Even more importantly, what drives these skills is his great sensitivity for the human condition. This is a large factor, among others, in generating empathy in the viewer. These images are expressed in a cinematic sense both epic in scale or warmly intimate as the narrative impulse requires. His storytelling gifts are supported by organizing skills that allow him to assemble complex material into rich tapestries of visual event which draw the viewer in.

How he does all this is in the man himself. His vision goes beyond the purely technical skills every artist must have. His intuitions are informed by life experiences and are transmitted by some very special abilities. His marvelously sensitive line is a virtual seismograph of his feelings. Energetic and totally appropriate paint surfaces, coupled with the grace and mystery of expressive greys and strong value contrasts are enchanting.

Herb's gentle yet forceful visions add a fresh, contemporary dimension to the body of great work in the Society of Illustrators Hall of Fame, and his future production is much anticipated.

Bob Levering

"The Trail of Tears," depicting the relocation of the Cherokee Indians from Georgia to Oklahoma, for *National Geographic*; charcoal on canvas and mixed media.

Anton Otto Fischer painted the sea with the authority of a seaman who had been there and lived it. Which he had.

Born in 1882 near Munich, Germany, orphaned at an early age, he was shunted from one unwilling relative to another for several years until at age sixteen he finally decided to break away on his own. Convinced by a poster advertising the glamorous life of a sailor, he prevailed on his unsympathetic uncle for permission to sign on to a small sailing vessel as an apprentice seaman. It was a cramped, ugly, ungainly craft known as a galleass, and he was too seasick on the whole first trip to perform his duties.

Eventually, he learned on the job, progressing to better ships and more responsibility. Not that better ships meant better food or lighter duties. It was the day of the wind-jammer and crossing from the Atlantic to the Pacific was still "around the Horn," one of the world's worst passages.

After eight years at sea, he left his ship in New York and applied for his first citizenship papers. He also found a summer job as a hand on a racing yacht on Long Island Sound. By chance, he read an ad offering a post as handyman and model for the illustrator, A.B. Frost. Being accepted for that job was the big break of his life. He was introduced to the milieu of a real artist—literally sleeping in the studio. Having drawn or sketched compulsively for years—without formal training—he wanted to try to change careers. Although he did not receive private instruction from Frost, he was encouraged in his spare-time efforts, and when the Frosts decided to go to Paris where Frost's sons were to go to art school, Fischer decided to go, too. He enrolled at the famous Academy Julian where he soaked in the art student's life for two years, until his funds ran out.

Upon his return to the States, he made a single marine painting as a sample, intending to take it around to the magazines. However, he sold it at his first call at *Harper's Weekly* and soon found further work from other magazines. *Everybody's* magazine teamed him with Jack London's stories, a prestigious break for a young illustrator. He was also a regular contributor to *The Saturday Evening Post*, an association that lasted for some forty years. Many book and magazine editors called on him when they wanted authenticity. He knew all the sailing ships and

their riggings and could paint rusty freighters or trim naval vessels with equal authority. He also could paint the ship's crews with the same understanding, recording the sea roll of their gait, the lived-in bagginess at the knees and elbows of their garb and the unshaven hairiness of weeks spent at sea.

For many years Fischer illustrated the popular sea stories of Guy Gilpatrick based on the rowdy crew of the freighter, "Inchliffe Castle," with Glencannon, the alcoholic Scottish ship's engineer as an unlikely hero. He was also the original illustrator for the redoubtable "Tugboat Annie" whose adventures he painted for an equal number of years.

Because of his German name, Fischer suffered from a considerable amount of patriotic prejudice during World War I. He dropped the "Otto" from his signature and moved to the Catskills where his foreign ancestry and accent would not be so conspicuous.

During World War II, he precluded any such prejudice by signing on as an official war artist with the Coast Guard and did sea duty on the U.S. Coast Guard Cutter, "Campbell," which was assigned to escort freighters on the North Atlantic run. There he saw considerable action with U-Boats which he recorded in a series of excellent paintings. His story and the paintings were published by *Life* magazine and credited to his full name and rank as Lt. Commander Anton Otto Fischer.

Following the war, he wrote and painted the pictures for *Fo'c'sle Days*, a book about his early adventures at sea. His career as a sailor had come along at the time when sail was giving way to steam and with working experience in both modes, he was able to recreate either with artistic insight. Because he knew about the bolts and rivets, the rope riggings and cuts of canvas, he could give them their due, but unlike some marine painters, he did not feel compelled to include all the minute detail and sacrifice the larger atmospheric setting of the weather and its elemental influence on the sea itself. It was this nice balance that made him one of the finest illustrators and painters of the sea.

Walt Reed
Illustration House

"Tugboat Annie," story by Norman Reilly Raine for *The Saturday Evening Post*, 1935. Permanent Collection of the Society of Illustrators Museum of American Illustration.

As a boy growing up in Michigan, Winsor McCay was influenced by an art teacher who stressed the value of perspective. Thereafter—in cartoons, comic strips, editorial cartoons, and animation (where many inventions were his but he refused to copyright them)—his astonishing, detailed drawings were infused with an atmosphere of depth and realism. There were other influences too: Art Nouveau decoration; stained-glass and poster-style outlining of figures; voguish colorings of rose, mauve, and olive; and a fascination with romantic and fantastic themes.

Dreams were the province of Winsor McCay—daydreams and nightmares, the fantasies of youth, idle speculations, the tantalizing fears of unknown realms. In virtually all of his cartoon work, dreams of fantasy formed the core, and none more so than in his classic masterpiece *Little Nemo in Slumberland*.

Commencing in 1905, *Little Nemo* added to the nascent art form some elements that no one before had contributed...and few have matched since. When the art form of the comic strip was a scant decade old, McCay took the basic elements of sequential panels and balloon-encased dialogue and committed himself to graphic excellence where others drew funny pictures; he wrote continuing stories where others conceived quick gags; he used a full palette where others colored between the lines.

When Little Nemo was born, newspaper color printing capabilities were at their highest point of development. *The New York Herald*'s color pages—produced by craftsmen who hand-tooled the plates and printed with an array of colored inks—have been unmatched in their vivid brilliance to this day.

Little Nemo, a weekly color page about a boy's continuing dreams, was a realistically drawn adventure about an absolutely fantastic world—a perfect juxtaposition for a comic strip, and a contrast to most strips, which depict everyday life in graphic whimsy.

The dreams of Nemo, a little boy of about six, beheld his bed walking, running, growing, flying, and floating. Nemo invariably journeyed to Slumberland where he initially sought the companionship of the lovely Princess, journeyed to meet her august father King Morpheus, and tried to avoid (finally consigning himself to suffering) the presence of the mischievous Flip.

In one of Nemo's memorable adventures he and his friends found themselves in Befuddle Hall, a palace where the laws of gravity were repealed: they walked on ceilings one week, on walls the next; and kaleidoscopic or fun-house mirrors enveloped reality. In another sequence Nemo visited the urban slum of Shantytown and, like a savior, transformed squalor to paradise and healed sick and dying children.

In his day McCay was a star of the vaudeville circuit, with Little Nemo the focus of lightning chalk-talks. There were reprint books of *Little Nemo in Slumberland* Sunday pages, a lavish 1908 Broadway operetta (with music by Victor Herbert), handsome Raphael Tuck postcards, and other manifestations of McCay's art and the public's adoration of it. Besides his many popular animated cartoons (like *Gertie the Dinosaur* and *Sinking of the Lusitania*) McCay was known for his many editorial cartoons, which often filled up half a newspaper page in the Hearst newspaper chain. McCay's powerful themes thundered like Old Testament prophecies on the subjects of morality, greed, sloth, and faith. He clearly enjoyed the influence he wielded...but he frequently stated that the Slumberland he created for Little Nemo was his first love.

Richard Marschall
President,
The National Foundation for Caricature and Cartoon Art

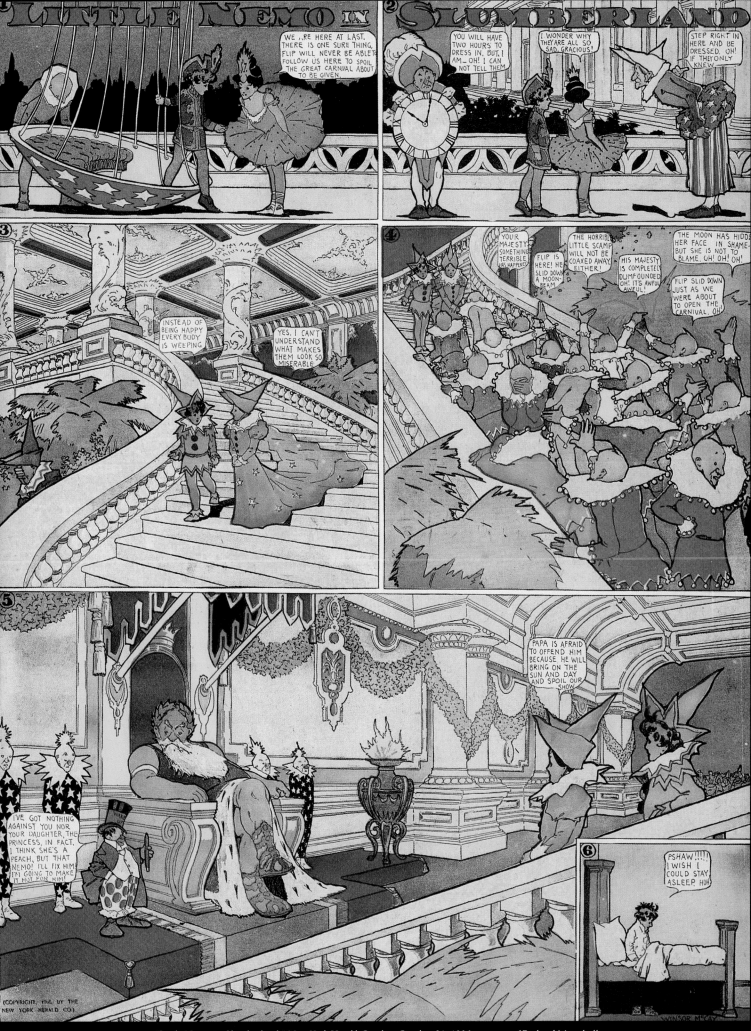

"Little Nemo in Slumberland," *New York Herald*, Sunday, October 21, 1906, courtesy of Richard Marschall

Violet Oakley was a strong willed, young woman with an independent streak when she began her career as an illustrator in Philadelphia in the late 1890s. Coming from an artistic family, she had already traveled widely in Europe, studying in Paris with the Symbolist painter Edmond Aman-Jean and with Charles Lazar in England. Her aunts Julianna and Isabella Oakley had lived abroad and studied painting in Munich and Florence. They sent home replicas of Old Master paintings that Violet recopied. According to family legend, it was a replica of Gainsborough's Mrs. Siddons that influenced Violet's decision to study painting.

Growing up in Bergen Heights, New Jersey, Violet began her training at the Art Students League in New York City taking classes with Carroll Beckwith and Irving Wiles. Subsequently moving with her family to Philadelphia, she studied portraiture with Cecilia Beaux at the Pennsylvania Academy of the Fine Arts. In 1897 she joined Howard Pyle's illustration class at the Drexel Institute. Having to supplement her family income due to her father's fragile health, she embarked on a career as an illustrator. With Pyle's encouragement, she made watercolor drawings for a new edition of Longfellow's Evangeline: A Tale of Acadie (1897), while her fellow student Jessie Willcox Smith drew the decorative headings.

Other book and magazine commissions followed, notably for Collier's Weekly, Century, Ladies' Home Journal, Everybody's, and St. Nicholas, a children's magazine. In addition, Violet supplied drawings for the Philadelphia Press newspaper; one was a full-page drawing for an issue memorializing President McKinley after his assassination in 1901. At the St. Louis Universal Exposition in 1904, she received a gold medal for illustration.

As in the work of other women illustrators of her day, women and children figured prominently in her pictures. On a Ladies' Home Journal Thanksgiving issue cover, a heroic Indian maiden carries a bountiful harvest of fruit while striding through a field of corn shocks and pumpkins. In another design young girls in flowing white dresses frolic in a meadow while picking flowers. Other illustrations show young women travelers resting on a hill overlooking a placid valley, a young girl and boy peering at a large book of Christmas tales held by Santa, and women conversing in the garden while waiting for tea. The subjects are of civilized, cultured people and appealed to the typical magazine reader.

While preparing an illustration, Violet selected models, arranged props, and photographed the scene. The camera provided an instant sketch from which she developed her final picture. For example, in a 1902 Collier's cover, four women raise their glasses of milk in a toast while seated at a table adorned by a teapot, cups, and glass milk bottles. This subject is directly based on a photograph taken at her studio that shows Violet and three other female friends in similar poses. One notable difference is that the wine bottles and beer steins shone in the photograph are replaced in the Collier's cover by the teapot and cups. Clearly, the cover of a family magazine could not show women drinking anything but milk or tea! Was the photograph Violet's way of showing women assuming a "bohemian" pose usually attributed to male artists?

The technique Violet used combined watercolor, crayon, and ink. She applied crayon broadly to textured paper, creating patterns of light and dark. She drew an outline around each figure separating them from the background. And she paid special attention to the decorative borders framing her drawings.

Violet Oakley's career as an illustrator was short-lived, lasting less than ten years. In 1900, after receiving a commission to design stained glass windows, a glass mosaic, and murals for the All Angels Church in New York City, her career objective switched to mural painting. In 1902 she was awarded a major mural commission to decorate the Pennsylvania State Capitol in Harrisburg. This marked the beginning of her productive career as a mural painter. In the 1930s she became active in the Women's International League for Peace and Freedom founded by Jane Addams, a Quaker feminist. During World War II, Violet painted twenty-five portable altarpieces for the Citizen's Committee for the Army and Navy. Also, she made portraits of the delegates to the League of Nations.

Violet Oakley told a newspaper reporter from the Baltimore Sun that she was surely "a monk in some earlier existence." Asked why a monk instead of a nun, she replied, "No, the abbesses and sisters were too busy nursing the sick and doing fine needleworks. I never heard of them illuminating manuscripts. I am quite sure I was a monk."

Elizabeth Hawkes
Independent Curator, West Chester, PA

THE COMPLETED
KING'S MOST
SET FORTH WITH THE
LICENCE
FALSE TO FAYETHE." — ANNE ASKEW CONDEMNED TO BE
REFUSING TO

"The Holy Experiment," study for a mural design. Courtesy of Illustration House.

Mead Schaeffer was born in Freedom Plains, New York, and grew up in Springfield, Massachusetts. He was the son of a Presbyterian minister, but called himself "a grandchild of Howard Pyle." On his walls were clippings of Howard Pyle's pirates. Intent on becoming an artist, he enrolled in Pratt Institute and began getting illustration jobs even before graduating. He studied with Dean Cornwell, a pupil of Harvey Dunn, and while working as a model for Cornwell and Dunn he submitted his work for Cornwell's criticism. "I didn't want any pay, I just wanted him to judge my samples. This is the way I broke in."

From this educational lineage, Schaeffer developed his talent in the finest tradition of the Brandywine School. "We were fortunate; we were in that marvelous period of Howard Pyle and everything grew out of him." N.C. Wyeth was another influence on Schaeffer and it showed in his portrayals of serious, powerfully built men. His friend Norman Rockwell saw Schaef as a slight, agile man who had a tremendous ability for painting the powerful, broad-shouldered, heroic man. Schaeffer's early illustrations of romance and adventure stories were characterized by a painterly style. This was painting that the viewer could sense viscerally, paint laid down in generous and satisfying strokes.

In 1922 Schaeffer's book illustrations for *Moby Dick*, the first in a series of 16 classics for Dodd Mead and Company, were published. Success and financial reward followed. By the time he illustrated *Les Miserables* in 1925, Schaeffer's technique had developed. His characters became more dimensional and more refined. He had mastered the rendering of texture, whether it was a stone cathedral, the rough deck of a ship, or the opalescence of sea foam— and one could feel his confidence in handling color. Brush strokes were executed with such sureness they became even thicker and more impressionistic. He invited the viewer to consider, not only the narrative of the image, but also the artist's tactile relationship to the canvas.

While still in his twenties, Schaeffer was contributing to the major magazines of the day. His work was featured in 19 magazines, including *McCall's*, *Cosmopolitan*, *American Magazine*, *Good Housekeeping*, *Harper's*, *Collier's*, *St. Nicholas*, *The Saturday Evening Post*, and *Woman's Home Companion*. At one point he was the highest paid illustrator in the country. Surprisingly, he never had a written contract with any magazine. "They were all gentlemen," he said, "it was a gentleman's agreement. If I liked the guy, I'd work my tail off." Although he did advertising illustrations, he didn't like doing them. "They held your brush for you."

In the late '30s, Schaeffer and Rockwell, both living in New Rochelle, met through phone conversations. They were using the same model, Fred Hildebrandt, and would call each other to schedule the sessions. Later, when Rockwell moved to Arlington, Vermont, Schaeffer also relocated there. He bought a house on the Green River where, at the end of his painting day, he could be found casting for brown trout. In Rockwell's autobiography, he recalled, "I had a stuffed owl in my studio. The poor old bird had a bare rump because Schaef was always plucking out the fluff under its tail to use in his dry flies. `Get away from there!,' I'd yell, catching, out of the corner of my eye, a glimpse of Schaef edging toward my owl." In addition to Rockwell, Arlington offered the company of Jack Atherton and George Hughes, two other *Post* cover artists. Peter Rockwell says only two opinions "really mattered" to his father—his mother's and Mead Schaeffer's.

Between 1942 and 1953, Schaeffer produced 45 *Post* covers. The first 14, the Armed Forces Commemorative Series, pictured each combat unit in action. The military sent servicemen to his studio to pose and the paintings toured the country to help sell war bonds. As his work became more reportorial and reality-based, Schaeffer traveled, saturating himself with material and absorbing the atmospheres for his picture. "If you haven't seen it, you haven't felt it, so obviously you can't paint it convincingly." In 1945, the *Post* sent Schaeffer and Rockwell out West on a two-and-a-half-month trip to gain inspiration for their cover work and that journey resulted in six covers from Schaeffer.

As a break from the insularity of Vermont, the Schaeffers spent each winter at Manthattan's Hotel des Artistes. Restless for the mainstream, Schaeffer left Arlington in 1950. Most of his remaining years were spent in Sea Cliff, New York, where he changed his painting medium to watercolor and "flirted" with abstractions. On November 6, 1980, while lunching at the Society of Illustrators, Schaeffer collapsed and died. The art of illustration, inspired and nourished by the Golden Age illustrators, was practiced and perfected by Mead Schaeffer—the "slight" man, painter of robust adventurers, creator of over 5,000 illustrations.

Linda Szekely
Assistant Curator
The Norman Rockwell Museum at Stockbridge

"Blue Roadster," Permanent Collection of the Society of Illustrators Museum of American Illustration.

The Hamilton King Award, created by Mrs. Hamilton King in memory of her husband through a bequest, is presented annually for the best illustration of the year by a member of the Society. The selection is made by former recipients of this award and may be won only once.

Also, the Society of Illustrators presents Special Awards each year for substantial contributions to the profession. The Dean Cornwell Recognition Award honors someone for past service which has proven to have been an important contribution to the Society. The Arthur William Brown Achievement Award honors someone who has made a substantial contribution to the Society over a period of time.

Paul Calle 1965

Bernie Fuchs 1966

Mark English 1967

Robert Peak 1968

Alan E. Cober 1969

Ray Ameijide 1970

Miriam Schottland 1971

Charles Santore 1972

Dave Blossom 1973

Fred Otnes 1974

Carol Anthony 1975

Judith Jampel 1976

Leo & Diane Dillon 1977

Daniel Schwartz 1978

William Teason 1979

Wilson McLean 1980

Gerald McConnell 1981

Robert Heindel 1982

Robert M. Cunningham 1983

Braldt Bralds 1984

Attila Hejja 1985

Doug Johnson 1986

Kinuko Y. Craft 1987

James McMullan 1988

Guy Billout 1989

Edward Sorel 1990

Brad Holland 1991

Gary Kelley 1992

Jerry Pinkney 1993

John Collier 1994

C.F. Payne 1995

Etienne Delessert 1996

1996 ARTHUR WILLIAM BROWN ACHIEVEMENT AWARD
Robert Hallock (1914-1982)

Portrait by Bernie Fuchs

From Bob Hallock I learned of his love of weather vanes, jazz, his 1765 house, and, of course, his charming wife Marian and their two children, John and Susan. I also learned of his serious and real dedication to art and graphic design. It was a privilege to know and work with Bob, whom I met through our efforts on the Society's behalf.

Hallock's career covered 46 years. He spread himself across the broad creative spectrum, from artist to art director to editor. The disciplines in which he worked included magazines, books, packaging, murals, exhibitions, stamp design, and films. He sought perfection in each of these endeavors, always with taste, and a love of art.

Hallock helped set the tone and overall look of all the Society's Annuals with his design of the first Society of Illustrators Annual book in 1959. Starting with that very first book and ending with the 24th edition in 1981, Bob completed seven of these Herculean tasks. All of Hallock's Annuals featured his special very sophisticated layout and design, and exhibited his great taste in type selection and picture placement. In the Society's first Annual, with only a few full-color pieces to work with, Hallock turned out the standard that was to be followed for years. *Illustrators 23*, the first full-color book, was also assigned to Hallock, and again he proved his skill at arriving at the perfect solution.

Hallock's greatest contribution to the field of illustration was in the graphic arts and public affairs journal, *Lithopinion*, which, starting in 1965, he brought to national attention. Acting as managing editor and art director of the quarterly, Hallock won over a hundred awards for excellence, including the prestigious New York State Council of the Arts Award, presented by Governor Rockefeller at the Metropolitan Museum of Art. *Lithopinion* showcased the best illustrators of the day—teaming them up with top writers, and helped to raise the illustration profession to new heights at a time in America when other media were vying for the illustrator's audience. In the ten years that Hallock managed *Lithopinion*, he proved that his constant quest for perfection and his unerring taste could gain positive attention for the profession.

For these reasons the Society has chosen to honor Robert Hallock as one of its most outstanding members. I know Bob would have been very proud to have received this award from his peers.

Jerry McConnell
Chairman, Publications Committee

1996 DEAN CORNWELL RECOGNITION AWARD
Jellybean Photographics

All illustrators and all art departments relish their best suppliers: their favorite FedEx driver, the shop with the all-night fax machine, the best computer store in town. They're like what the trusted plumber is to a home owner.

And for every illustrator and art department a very special supplier is needed before art can be reproduced— the photo house. In New York—a small city, graphically speaking— every day one can see the portfolios, vans and bike messengers of one of the very few good photo houses—a quaint reminder that a pulse and fast pedals are often as important as a web site.

This locally ubiquitous logo belongs to Jellybean Photographics. Not only are they shooters for the stars— top illustrators, that is—but they are also keenly aware of the continuity of the business. To that end they generously support the Society's Scholarship efforts.

Jellybean's annual grants for the past twelve years have funded awards in the Annual Student Scholarship Competition. With matching grants, Jellybean's support has totaled over $64,000—credential enough to warrant a Special Award.

Beyond the fiscal largesse, Jellybean speaks out among the other ancillary businesses to the creative arts and says, "Hey, we should all be doing our part for the new, young artists as they enter the real world wet behind the ears." Jellybean has done its part for over twenty-one students from thirteen colleges in the New York Metropolitan area in the past dozen years.

Jellybean Photographics—now, there's a great name for a supplier. Behind the candy coat-of-arms is an effective businesswoman: Geri Bauer. Geri started the company twenty years ago and today the Jellybean logo is a "byte" in the collective illustration RAM. Geri also carries an enthusiastic interest in African wildlife and supports the William Holden Wildlife Foundation. She has lunched frequently at the Society with Stephanie Powers to discuss that foundation's work.

In the commercial world, no part of the creative process goes it alone. Either you need FedEx or Fred's Fax or Phil's Floppies. And if you are in the New York area and need a good photo house, just look between the cabs and sooner or later you'll see the Jellybean logo. It's user friendly and students are welcome!

Terrence Brown
Director, Society of Illustrators

Most of my favorite artists are dead. There are several advantages to this. The main one is I don't keep running into them at openings. Having to choose between perfection of the work and of the life, the best artists are often duds when you meet them. But I loved Etienne Delessert's work before I met him, and now that I know him, I can tell you that his pictures are his heart and soul made visible.

I first saw Etienne's drawings in 1967. That summer he illustrated an entire issue of *Fact Magazine*. *Fact* was one of those centaurs of sixties journalism: half *Consumer Reports*, half *National Enquirer*. Its articles "exposed" the evils of drinking Coke, voting for George Romney, and reading the *Reader's Digest*. But neither the magazine's squishy politics nor its rock-em, sock-em prose engaged me the way Etienne's simple ink drawings did. Crosshatched with the delicacy of drybrush and designed with the boldness of flags, they sat on the page like Rorschach tests. A quarter century later, they've outlasted the articles they were meant to play second fiddle to.

They've lasted, not because Etienne, the trusty illustrator, played Tonto to the assignment--but because he used the assignment to focus his imagination on the themes behind the words. Twenty-nine years later he paints pictures for exhibitions in a similar way.

He sets himself a problem which instead of attacking headlong, he flanks, inventing variations on a theme as if he were deploying ants to surround a boulder.

This picture, which was voted the Hamilton King Award this year, is one of thirty on a subject he called "Little Lights of Paradise." The title reflects his upbringing as a preacher's kid in Lausanne, Switzerland. Unlike his Calvinist father, Etienne believes that paradise is no more than "an existential carrot," a little trick the soul plays on its material self, without which most people would find life "too sad to endure." Yet he sees the simple pleasures and insights of life as a kind of cosmic night light. The catalogue for the exhibition illuminates (so-to-speak) this idea.

The pictures were painted in acrylic on tin, a technique Etienne adapted from Seymour Chwast's painted tin sculptures. Rendered in blacks and grays and burgundies, the darkness of each is warmed by a faint aura. Sometimes it's a glow like fireflies in a jar; sometimes it's the dim blur of foxfire, the luminescence of decay. These are religious pictures without theology. Paintings of faith without belief.

Of course individuals may, but no society has ever existed for long without a shared belief in something. For Etienne it seems the "little light" of his craftsmanship does the trick. But in our New Age of nurturing angels and swamis doing infomercials fewer people accept the fact that most of life's problems are too fundamental to be solved by anything as temporary as life.

For Etienne salvation is a practical matter. It's the boulder we can never occupy but only surround with our inventions--to keep ourselves busy and give ourselves delight. His distorted figures are lumps of clay, who for a moment in eternity are able to sit up and realize that they're lumps of clay. This candle watt of self-awareness is their salvation. And Etienne uses the stimulus of this conceit to invent characters as cartoonish and tragic as the stoic blue warriors in Aztec sacrificial murals.

It's appropriate that I first saw his work in the 1960s, the decade in which fine artists began turning comic strip panels into gallery paintings. The campiness of Pop Art gave symmetry to the work of this self-taught preacher's kid who was bringing the intensity of fine art to cartoons. And it proves again that the old question about what's fine art and what's illustration, however relevant--is never decisive. No form of art ever has its authority conferred by definition. The pop artists of the sixties were cynics paying homage to sentimentality. Etienne was and is a folk artist. He applies his talent to popular culture with the directness and authority of a child who, having matured at a young age, has been permitted by the bargain to stay young indefinitely.

Brad Holland

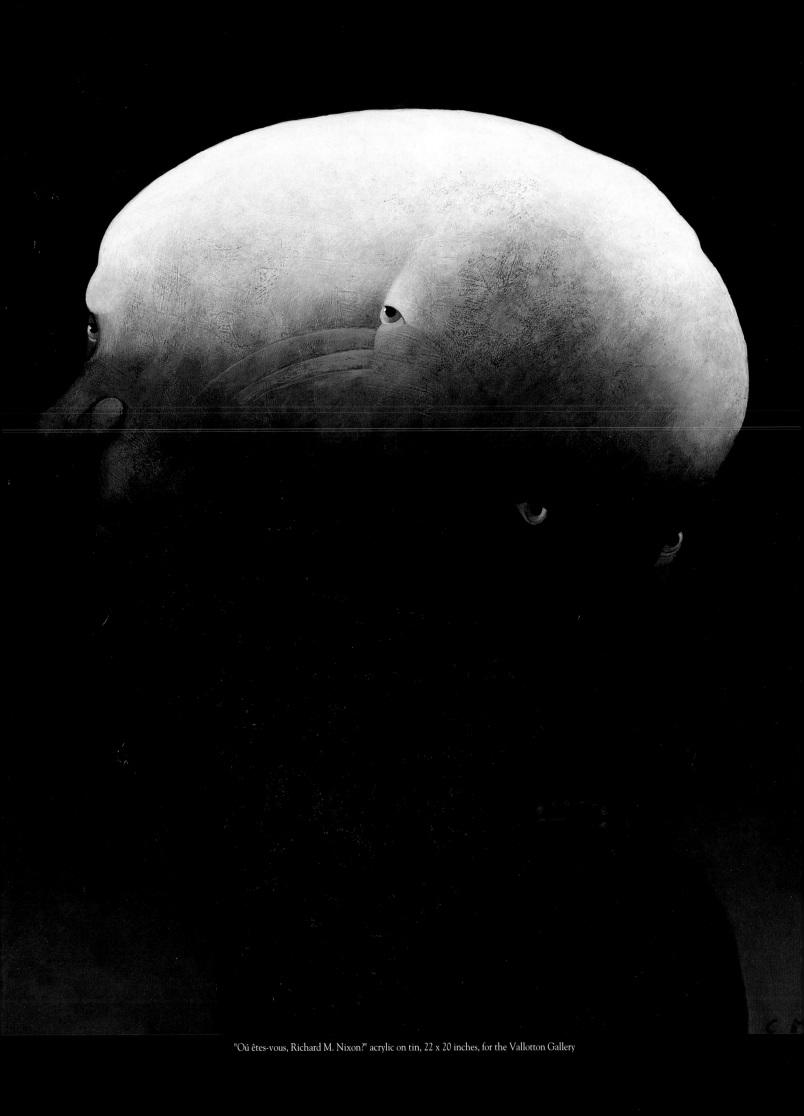

"Oú êtes-vous, Richard M. Nixon?" acrylic on tin, 22 x 20 inches, for the Vallotton Gallery

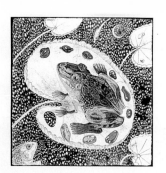

Portrait by Brad Holland

SOCIETY
of ILLUSTRATORS
38th ANNUAL
EXHIBITION
CALL for ENTRIES
DEADLINE
OCTOBER 2, 1995

EDITORIAL & BOOK
CATEGORIES EXHIBITION:
FEBRUARY 10 to MARCH 9, 1996
ADVERTISING & INSTITUTIONAL
CATEGORIES EXHIBITION:
MARCH 16 to APRIL 13, 1996

With the publication of the *38th Annual of American Illustration* by the Society of Illustrators, the completion of my tenure as Chairman has been reached. This time has been nothing less than a dream come true. I gladly accepted the job because of my fondness and deep appreciation for what the Society of Illustrators represents to me and other illustrators. I'll admit I was a little apprehensive about the challenge that lay ahead, but the Society's staff vanquished all fears and made the job a slam dunk.

This *38th Annual of American Illustration* is deeply indebted to a boatload of talented and giving individuals, from Jack Unruh, who illustrated our Call for Entries and Jack Summerford, who designed it, to Fred Woodward, the designer of the cover of this book, and Brad Holland, whose illustration was selected for it. I am particularly proud of the Jury Chairs and their respective juries for their professionalism and dedication to the jurying process. It was a pleasure and an honor to work with these fine people.

As you turn the pages of this annual, I hope you will find a Society of Illustrators that is extending a hand to all illustrators. The dynamics of our industry are changing rapidly, with illustrators now having the ability to live and work anywhere—we run the risk of being more and more fractionalized. Yet the Society of Illustrators is always there. I believe this annual reaches out, making a call to all illustrators that it is your home. I know some illustrators did not enter this show; I can only hope they will reconsider in future years. Many congratulations to those represented and rewarded by the *38th Annual of American Illustration*.

C.F. Payne
Chairman, 38h Annual Exhibition

ILLUSTRATORS

EDITORIAL JURY

MARK HESS
CHAIRMAN
Illustrator, Stamp Designer

LOU DORFSMAN
Creative Director, Design,
Museum of Television and Radio

REGAN DUNNICK
Illustrator

ROBERT GIUSTI
Illustrator, Graphic Designer

GREGORY MANCHESS
Illustrator

HOWARD PAINE
Art Director

ROBERT ANDREW PARKER
Illustrator

LYNN PAULEY
Illustrator

DOUG SMITH
Smith Concept and Design, Illustration,
Product/Package Design

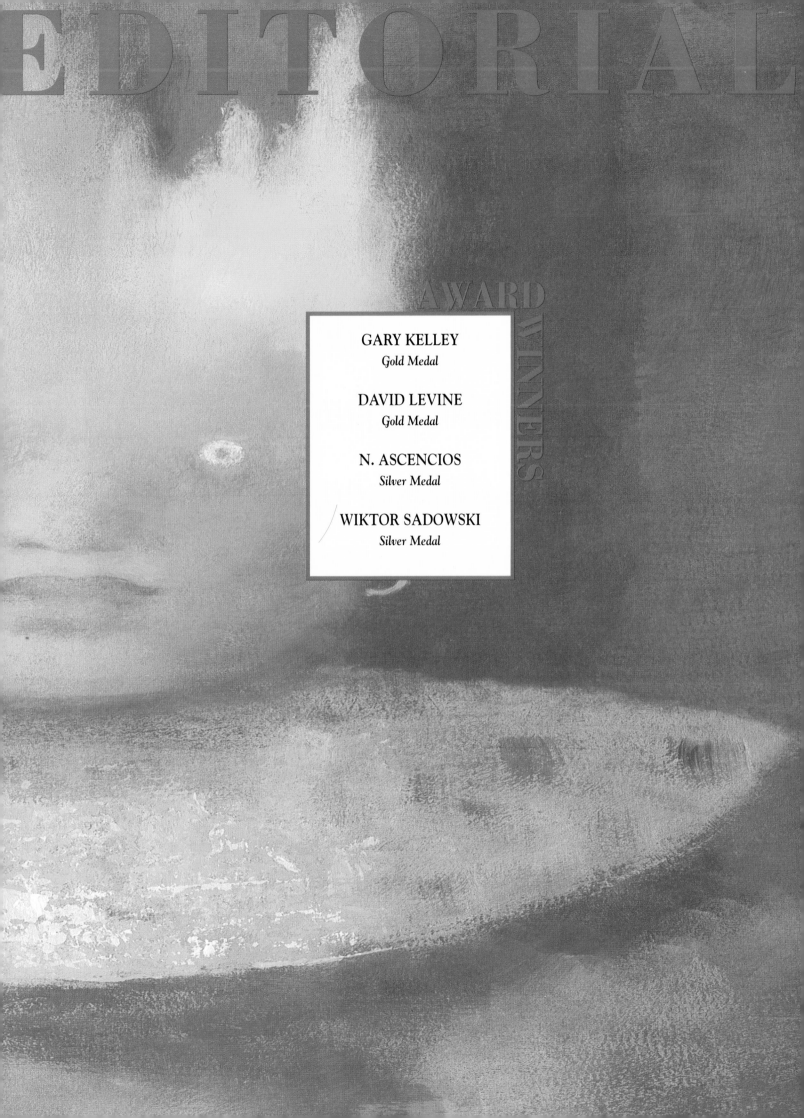

AWARD WINNERS

GARY KELLEY
Gold Medal

DAVID LEVINE
Gold Medal

N. ASCENCIOS
Silver Medal

WIKTOR SADOWSKI
Silver Medal

1

Artist: **GARY KELLEY**

Art Director: Andy Kner

Client: Scenario Magazine

Medium: Pastel on paper

Size: 20" x 17"

Editorial Gold Medal
GARY KELLEY

"I'd like to thank the Society for this award, my friend Honk for posing even though he doesn't play the guitar, and my wife Linda for posing even though she doesn't smoke."

1

2

Artist: **DAVID LEVINE**

Art Director: Chris Curry

Client: The New Yorker

Size: 10" x 7"

Editorial Gold Medal
DAVID LEVINE

For this drawing, which accompanied the release of a part of Phillip Roth's new book, Levine took aim on a subject he has drawn before and, despite Mr. Roth's contention otherwise, made the nose just right. The transition from commercial work to painting—another aspect of his career—is not always easy, according to the artist. The thinking is different and there have been occasions when he returns to a half-finished canvas and wonders, "Who did that?"

3

Artist: **N. ASCENCIOS**

Art Directors: Arthur Hochstein
Kenneth Smith

Client: Time

Medium: Oil on canvas

Size: 12" x 10"

Editorial Silver Medal
N. ASCENCIOS

"N. Ascencios favors velvety forests where she works with her muses and has picnics with little monkeys. After eating melon, they put their culinary itinerary aside and play cards and chess, discuss ideas and perform/recite lyrical poetry. Despite varied tempers, on special days they work on commissioned paintings...minutes are replete with hours...until dawn. In the last seconds, Natalie surveys the painting and dresses it in rare satins, powdery silks and a wig with shiny curls. `It is ready...send it out,' she announces. The art, young and giddy, finally breaks into a puffy smile and feels ready to be scrutinized."

4

Artist: **WIKTOR SADOWSKI**

Art Director: Ginny Lams

Client: The Magazine of Golden Gate
University

Medium: Acrylic

Size: 11" x 8"

Editorial Silver Medal
WIKTOR SADOWSKI

This is Wiktor Sadowski's second medal from the Annual Show. He and others whose studios are beyond these borders have brought a fresh approach to illustration in America. For this illustration, all the artist had to work with was the title: "The Nature of Evil." In fact, the article had not yet been written when he got the assignment. The sketches reflected a human figure, not gender specific, and the snake was Wiktor's concept.

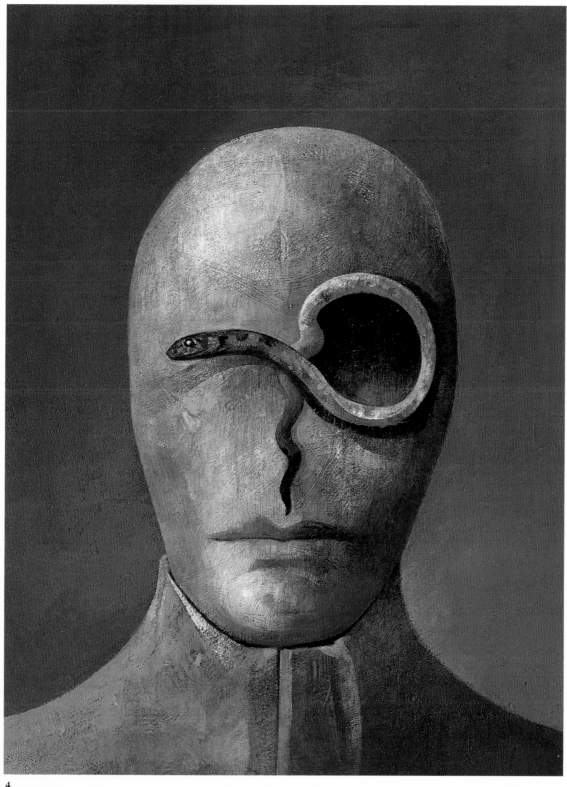

5

Artist: **ETIENNE DELESSERT**

Art Director: Steve Heller

Client: The New York Times Book Review

Medium: Watercolor

Size: 19" x 17"

6

Artist: **ISTVAN BANYAI**

Art Director: Tom Staebler

Client: Playboy

Medium: Ink on vinyl

Size: 11" x 14"

7

Artist: **MARK CHICKINELLI**

Art Director: Mark Chickinelli

Client: Workbook

Medium: Acrylic on board

Size: 13" x 7"

8

Artist: **PHILIP BURKE**

Art Director: David Harris

Client: Vanity Fair

Medium: Oil on canvas

Size: 3' x 4'

5

6

7

8

9

Artist: **MARSHALL ARISMAN**

Art Director: Janet Froelich

Client: The New York Times Magazine

Medium: Oil on ragboard

Size: 22" x 20"

10

Artist: **MARSHALL ARISMAN**

Art Director: Frank Devino

Client: Penthouse

Medium: Oil on ragboard

Size: 29" x 23"

11

Artist: **N. ASCENCIOS**

Art Director: Lee Bearson

Client: Rolling Stone

Medium: Oil on canvas

Size: 14" x 10"

12

Artist: **N. ASCENCIOS**

Art Director: Chris Curry

Client: The New Yorker

Medium: Oil on canvas

Size: 9" x 21"

9

10

11

12

13

Artist: **PETER MALONE**

Art Director: Chris Curry

Client: The New Yorker

Medium: Gouache on watercolor paper

Size: 5" x 5"

14

Artist: **VIVIENNE FLESHER**

Art Director: Tom Staebler

Client: Playboy

Medium: Pastel

15

Artist: **MARK SUMMERS**

Art Director: Steve Heller

Client: The New York Times Book Review

Medium: Scratchboard

Size: 12" x 7"

16

Artist: **MARK SUMMERS**

Art Director: Steve Heller

Client: The New York Times Book Review

Medium: Scratchboard

Size: 11" x 5 1/2"

13

14

George Eliot

15

Walt Whitman

16

17

Artist: **PHILIP BURKE**

Art Director: Chris Curry

Client: The New Yorker

Medium: Oil on canvas

Size: 3' x 4'

18

Artist: **DAVID CHRISTIANA**

Client: Omni

Medium: Oil

Size: 6" x 28"

19

Artist: **DAVID M. BECK**

Art Director: Robert Mason

Client: Review & Herald Publishing
        Assn.

Medium: Mixed on Strathmore

Size: 12" x 9"

20

Artist: **MIKE BENNY**

Art Director: Arthur Hochstein

Client: Time

Medium: Acrylic on board

Size: 18" X 12"

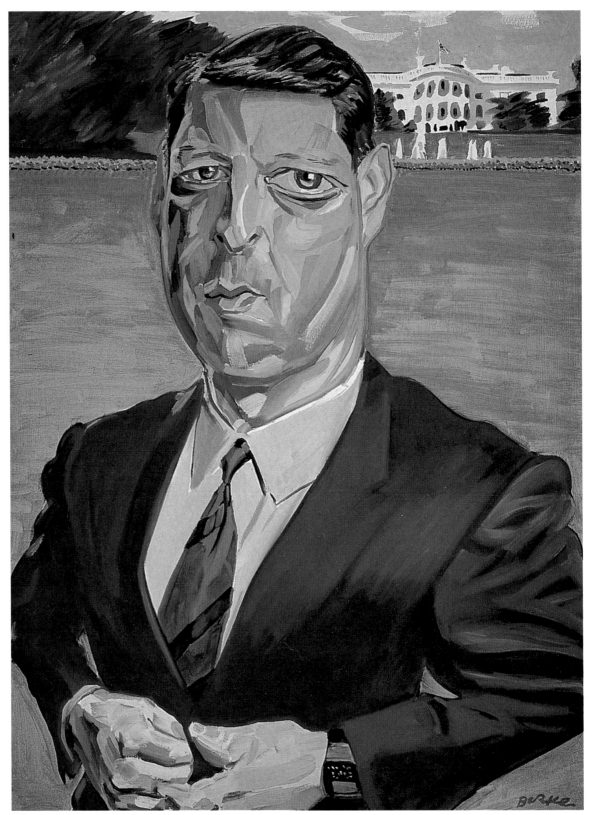

17

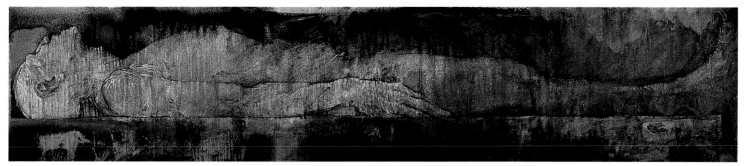

18

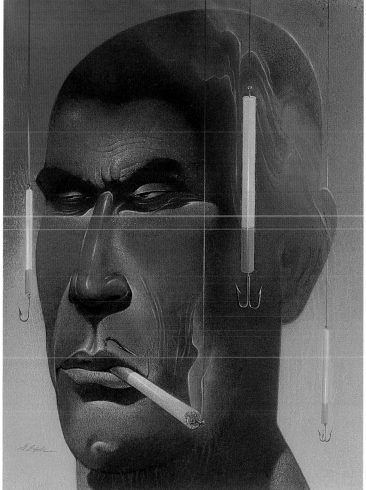

19

20

21

Artist: **MARK ENGLISH**

Art Director: Tim Trabon

Medium: Pastel

Size: 14" x 13"

22

Artist: **RANDY PALMER**

Art Director: Lee Waigand

Client: Dayton Daily News

Medium: Acrylic on board

Size: 9" x 9"

23

Artist: **MILTON GLASER**

Art Director: Al Braverman

Client: New Choices

Medium: Mixed

Size: 15" x 11"

24

Artist: **GREG HARLIN**

Art Director: Caroline Sheen

Client: Air & Space Magazine

Medium: Watercolor on board

Size: 7" x 3"

21

22

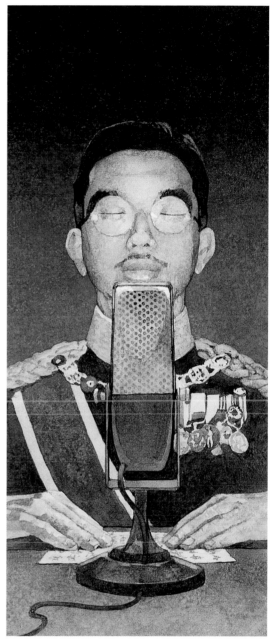

23

24

25

Artist: **ROBERT GIUSTI**

Art Director: Mary Workman

Client: The Atlantic Monthly

Medium: Acrylic on linen

Size: 13" x 10"

26

Artist: **MIKE BENNY**

Art Director: John Korpics

Client: GQ

Medium: Acrylic on board

Size: 18" x 14"

27

Artist: **DONALD BIED**

Medium: Acrylic on paper

Size: 17" x 13"

28

Artist: **DAVID M. BECK**

Art Director: Jef Capaldi

Client: American Medical News

Medium: Mixed on Strathmore

Size: 12 1/2" x 16"

26

27

28

29

Artist: **DAVID CHRISTIANA**

Art Director: Christine Butterworth

Client: Sycamore Review

Medium: Oil on canvas

Size: 84" x 60"

30

Artist: **PHIL BOATWRIGHT**

Art Director: Christine Mitchell

Client: Arizona Highways

Medium: Mixed on Strathmore board

Size: 10" x 14"

31

Artist: **TIM BORGERT**

Art Director: David Kordalski

Client: Dayton Daily News

Medium: Mixed on watercolor board

Size: 17" x 14"

32

Artist: **JOHN COLLIER**

Art Director: Mary Workman

Client: The Atlantic Monthly

Medium: Pastel, gouache

Size: 13" x 10"

30

31

32

33

Artist: **BRAD HOLLAND**

Art Director: Sam Shahid

Client: Mirabella

Medium: Acrylic on masonite

Size: 14" x 14"

34

Artist: **DARRELL D. MAYABB**

Art Director: Daniel Stout

Client: Airgroup Publishing

Medium: Gouache on Strathmore

Size: 15" x 18"

35

Artist: **BRAD HOLLAND**

Art Director: Kelly Doe

Client: The Washington Post Magazine

Medium: Acrylic on masonite

Size: 11" x 8 1/2"

36

Artist: **AMY NING**

Art Director: Tia Lai

Client: The Orange County Register

Medium: Acrylic, airbrush

Size: 10" x 9"

33

34

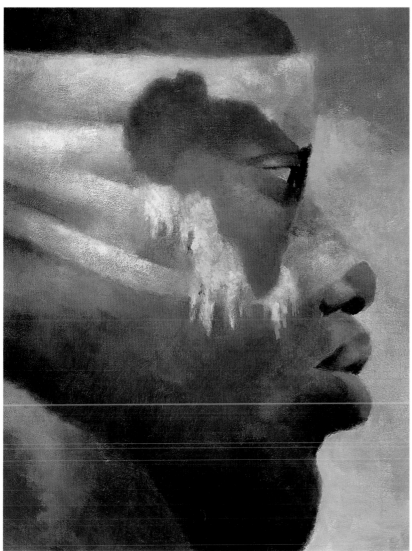

35

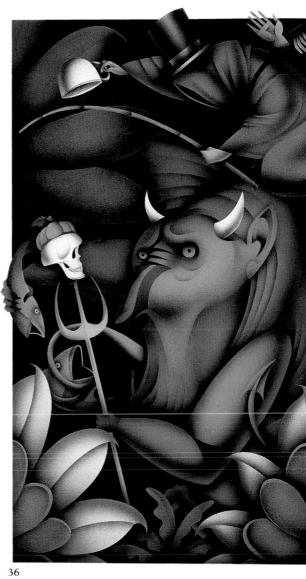

36

37

Artist: **JOHN COLLIER**

Art Director: Amid Capeci

Client: Esquire

Medium: Pastel

Size: 26" x 20"

38

Artist: **TIM BORGERT**

Art Director: David Kordalski

Client: Dayton Daily News

Medium: Mixed on watercolor board

Size: 11" x 17"

39

Artist: **BILL CIGLIANO**

Art Director: Robert Mason

Client: Listen

Medium: Oil, gouache on board

Size: 11" x 8"

40

Artist: **MARK BRAUGHT**

Art Director: Chris Willett

Client: Scholastic Inc.

Medium. Pastel

Size: 13" x 10"

37

38

39

40

41

Artist: **H.B. LEWIS**

Art Director: Andy Christy

Client: Forbes

Medium: Mixed on paper

Size: 11" x 11"

42

Artist: **WILSON McLEAN**

Art Director: Len Willis

Client: Playboy

Medium: Oil on canvas

Size: 24" x 24"

43

Artist: **PETER de SÈVE**

Art Director: Ed Rich

Client: Smithsonian Magazine

Medium: Watercolor, ink

44

Artist: **LARRY DAY**

Art Director: Larry Day

Client: Chicago Tribune Magazine

Medium: Watercolor, gouache on
watercolor paper

Size: 15" x 22"

41

42

43

44

45

Artist: **PETER de SÈVE**

Art Director: Francoise Mouly

Client: The New Yorker

Medium: Watercolor, ink

Size: 14" x 10"

46

Artist: **GREG HARLIN**

Art Director: Caroline Sheen

Client: Air & Space Magazine

Medium: Watercolor on board

Size: 6" x 7"

47

Artist: **PHIL BOATWRIGHT**

Art Director: Christine Mitchell

Client: Arizona Highways

Medium: Mixed on Strathmore board

Size: 17" x 13"

48

Artist: **RICHARD DOWNS**

Art Directors: Rip Georges
　　　　　　　Pamela Thornberg

Client: Los Angeles Magazine

Medium: Collaged monotype on
　　　　　Japanese hand made papers

Size: 21" x 16"

45

46

47

48

49

Artist: **MICHAEL PARASKEVAS**

Art Director: Wiley Nash

Client: Audacity

Medium: Acrylic

Size: 18" x 18"

50

Artist: **MICHAEL PARASKEVAS**

Art Director: Beth Lower

Client: Union

Medium: Acrylic

Size: 34" x 28"

51

Artist: **WILLIAM JOYCE**

Art Director: Steve Heller

Client: The New York Times

Medium: Oil on Bristol board

Size: 12" x 12"

52

Artist: **WILLIAM JOYCE**

Art Director: Steve Heller

Client: The New York Times

Medium: Oil on Bristol board

Size: 9" x 12"

49

50

51

52

53

Artist: **JAMES McMULLAN**

Art Director: Amid Capeci

Client: Esquire

Medium: Watercolor on paper

Size: 10" x 8"

54

Artist: **MILTON GLASER**

Art Director: Suzanne Morin

Client: Audubon

Medium: Mixed

Size: 14" x 11"

55

Artist: **MARK HESS**

Art Director: Barbara Dewilde

Client: Alfred A. Knopf

Medium: Acrylic on wood

Size: 19" x 13"

56

Artist: **MICHAEL GARLAND**

Medium: Oil on canvas

Size: 20" x 24"

53

54

55

56

57

Artist: **DAVID WILCOX**

Art Director: Len Willis

Client: Playboy

Medium: Vinyl, acrylic on board

Size: 19" x 19"

58

Artist: **KENT WILLIAMS**

Art Director: Tom Staebler

Client: Playboy

Medium: Oil on wood panel

Size: 22" x 22"

59

Artist: **JOHN KASCHT**

Art Director: Dolores Motichka

Client: The Washington Times

Medium: Watercolor on Strathmore board

Size: 17" x 11"

60

Artist: **JOHN KASCHT**

Art Director: Dolores Motichka

Client: The Washington Times

Medium: Watercolor on Strathmor board

Size: 18" x 13"

57

59

60

61

Artist: **BURT SILVERMAN**

Art Directors: Arthur Hochstein
Kenneth Smith

Client: Time

Medium: Oil on canvas

Size: 24" x 20"

62

Artist: **TIM SHEAFFER**

Art Director: David Harris

Client: Vanity Fair

Medium: Ink

Size: 15" x 11"

63

Artist: **DANIEL SCHWARTZ**

Art Director: Lori Wendin

Client: Tennis

Medium: Oil on canvas

Size: 20" x 16"

64

Artists: **STEVE JOHNSON
LOU FANCHER**

Art Director: Jason Krauss

Client: Chevy Outdoors

Medium: Acrylic on canvas

Size: 10" x 17 1/2"

61

62

63

64

65

Artist: **MARK STUTZMAN**

Art Director: Marianne Serif

Client: The World Future Society

Medium: Mixed

Size: 22" x 17"

66

Artist: **GARY KELLEY**

Art Director: Fred Woodward

Client: Rolling Stone

Medium: Pastel on paper

Size: 11" x 17"

67

Artist: **JOSEPH DANIEL FIEDLER**

Art Director: Seema Christie

Client: New Woman

Medium: Alkyd

Size: 13" x 9"

68

Artist: **ANDREA VENTURA**

Art Director: Robin Barnes

Client: The Atlantic Monthly

Medium: Acrylic, charcoal on paper

Size: 15" x 9"

65

66

67

68

69

Artist: **C.F. PAYNE**

Art Directors: Fred Woodward
Gail Anderson

Client: Rolling Stone

Medium: Mixed

Size: 8" x 8"

70

Artist: **DAVID JOHNSON**

Art Director: Robin Gilmore-Barnes

Client: The Atlantic Monthly

Medium: Pen & ink on paper

Size: 11" x 10"

71

Artist: **KAZUHIKO SANO**

Art Director: Daisuke Koga

Agency: Saurus Design

Client: Gakken Co., Ltd.

Medium: Acrylic on board

Size: 18" x 27"

72

Artist: **KAZUHIKO SANO**

Art Director: Daisuke Koga

Agency: Saurus Design

Client: Gakken Co., Ltd.

Medium: Acrylic on board

Size: 18" x 26"

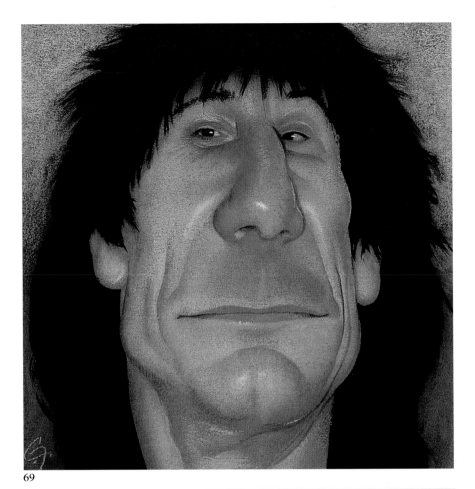

69

70

71

72

73

Artist: **JACK N. UNRUH**

Art Director: Kyle Dreier

Client: American Airlines

Medium: Ink, watercolor on board

Size: 20" x 15"

74

Artist: **LARA TOMLIN**

Art Director: Chris Curry

Client: The New Yorker

Medium: Hand colored etching
on Arches

Size: 9" x 6"

75

Artist: **GARY KELLEY**

Art Director: Fred Woodward

Client: Rolling Stone

Medium: Pastel on paper

Size: 15" x 11"

76

Artist: **KENNETH SMITH**

Medium: Oil on masonite

Size: 20" x 32"

73

74

75

76

77

Artist: **C.F. PAYNE**

Art Director: Tom Hawley

Client: Cincinnati Magazine

Medium: Mixed

Size: 17" x 12"

78

Artist: **DAHL TAYLOR**

Medium: Oil on canvas

Size: 30" x 48"

79

Artist: **VICTOR JUHASZ**

Art Director: Chris Curry

Client: The New Yorker

Medium: Watercolor, colored pencils
on bond paper

Size: 15" x 12"

80

Artist: **PHIL HULING**

Art Director: David Whitmore

Client: The Learning Channel
Monthly

Medium: Mixed

Size: 10" x 7"

78

79

80

81

Artist: **KRIS WILTSE**

Art Director: Stefanie Swannack

Client: Seattle

Medium: Block print

Size: 9" x 7"

82

Artist: **PHIL BOATWRIGHT**

Art Director: Jef Capaldi

Client: American Medical News

Medium: Mixed on Strathmore board

Size: 14" x 11"

83

Artist: **HERB TAUSS**

Art Director: Allen Carroll

Client: National Geographic

Medium: Oil, crayon, charcoal on canvas

Size: 34" x 44"

84

Artist: **JOE SORREN**

Art Directors: Joe Mitch
Joe Sorren

Client: Transworld Snowboarding Magazine

Medium: Acrylic on canvas

Size: 4' x 6'

81

82

83

84

85

Artist: **EDWARD SOREL**

Art Director: Francoise Mouly

Client: The New Yorker

Medium: Watercolor

Size: 22" x 16"

86

Artist: **DAVID TOMB**

Art Director: Owen Philips

Client: The New Yorker

Size: 23" x 20"

87

Artist: **RICHARD MERKIN**

Art Director: Chris Curry

Client: The New Yorker

Medium: Pastel, oil crayon on
hand made paper

Size: 41" x 32"

88

Artist: **ROBERT ANDREW
PARKER**

Art Director: Mary Workman

Client: The Atlantic Monthly

Medium: Monoprint

Size: 17" x 20"

85

86

87

88

89

Artist: **GREGORY MANCHESS**

Art Director: Cathryn Mezzo

Client: Omni

Medium: Oil on gesso

Size: 24" x 18"

90

Artist: **MICHAEL PARASKEVAS**

Art Director: Michael Paraskevas

Client: Dan's Paper

Medium: Acrylic on canvas

Size: 54" x 66"

91

Artist: **LOREN LONG**

Art Director: Craig Gartner

Client: Sports Illustrated

Medium: Acrylic on board

Size: 17" x 16"

92

Artist: **GREGORY MANCHESS**

Art Director: Christine Dunleavey

Client: The Philadelphia Inquirer Magazine

Medium: Oil on gesso

Size: 20" x 17"

89

90

91

92

93

Artist: **C.F. PAYNE**

Art Director: Arthur Hochstein

Client: Time

Medium: Mixed on board

Size: 14" x 11"

94

Artist: **MIRKO ILIC**

Art Director: Wayne Fitzpatrick

Client: Emerge

Medium: Scratchboard

Size: 14" x 10"

95

Artist: **LORENZO MATTOTTI**

Art Director: Francoise Mouly

Client: The New Yorker

Medium: Mixed

Size: 14" x 11"

96

Artist: **FRANCIS LIVINGSTON**

Client: Modern Maturity

Medium: Oil on board

Size: 18" x 11"

93

94

95

96

97

Artist: **KEITH GRAVES**

Art Director: Lance Pettiford

Client: YSB

Medium: Prismacolor, acrylic on board

Size: 14" x 12"

98

Artist: **ALAN E. COBER**

Art Director: Catie Aldrich

Client: The Boston Globe Magazine

Medium: Ink, watercolor

Size: 13" x 11"

99

Artist: **ROBERT HUNT**

Art Director: Ken Palumbo

Client: Bicycling Magazine

Medium: Oil, pastel

Size: 24" x 18"

100

Artist: **CARTER GOODRICH**

Art Director: Francoise Mouly

Client: The New Yorker

Medium: Watercolor, colored pencil on board

Size: 18" x 14"

97

98

99

100

101

Artist: **JOHN PATRICK**

Art Director: Tom Hawley

Client: Cincinnati Magazine

Medium: Gouache, watercolor on board

Size: 15" x 11"

102

Artist: **MATTHEW BANDSUCH**

Art Director: David Buffington

Client: HR Strategies

Medium: Acrylic on board

Size: 12" x 9"

103

Artist: **GREGORY MANCHESS**

Art Director: Chris Sloan

Client: National Geographic Society

Medium: Oil

Size: 24" x 34"

104

Artist: **PHILIP BURKE**

Art Director: Kerry Tremain

Client: Mother Jones

Medium: Oil on canvas

Size: 3' x 4'

101

102

103

104

105

Artist: **JAMES MARSH**

Art Director: Suzanne Morin

Client: Audubon Magazine

Medium: Acrylic on canvas

106

Artist: **ROBERT ANDREW PARKER**

Art Director: Arthur Hochstein

Client: Time

Medium: Monoprint

107

Artist: **ROBERT ANDREW PARKER**

Art Director: Arthur Hochstein

Client: Time

Medium: Monoprint

108

Artist: **BOB NEWMAN**

Client: Newsday

Medium: Iris Print

Size: 5" x 8"

105

106

107

108

BOOK JURY

MURRAY TINKELMAN
CHAIRMAN
Illustrator

KELLY DOE
Art Director
The Washington Post Magazine

BART FORBES
Illustrator

JUDY GARLAN
Art Director
The Atlantic Monthly

BRAD HOLLAND
Illustrator

TIM O'BRIEN
Illustrator

JAMES RANSOME
Illustrator

MADALINA STEFAN
Art Director
Scholastic Inc.

BARRON STOREY
Illustrator

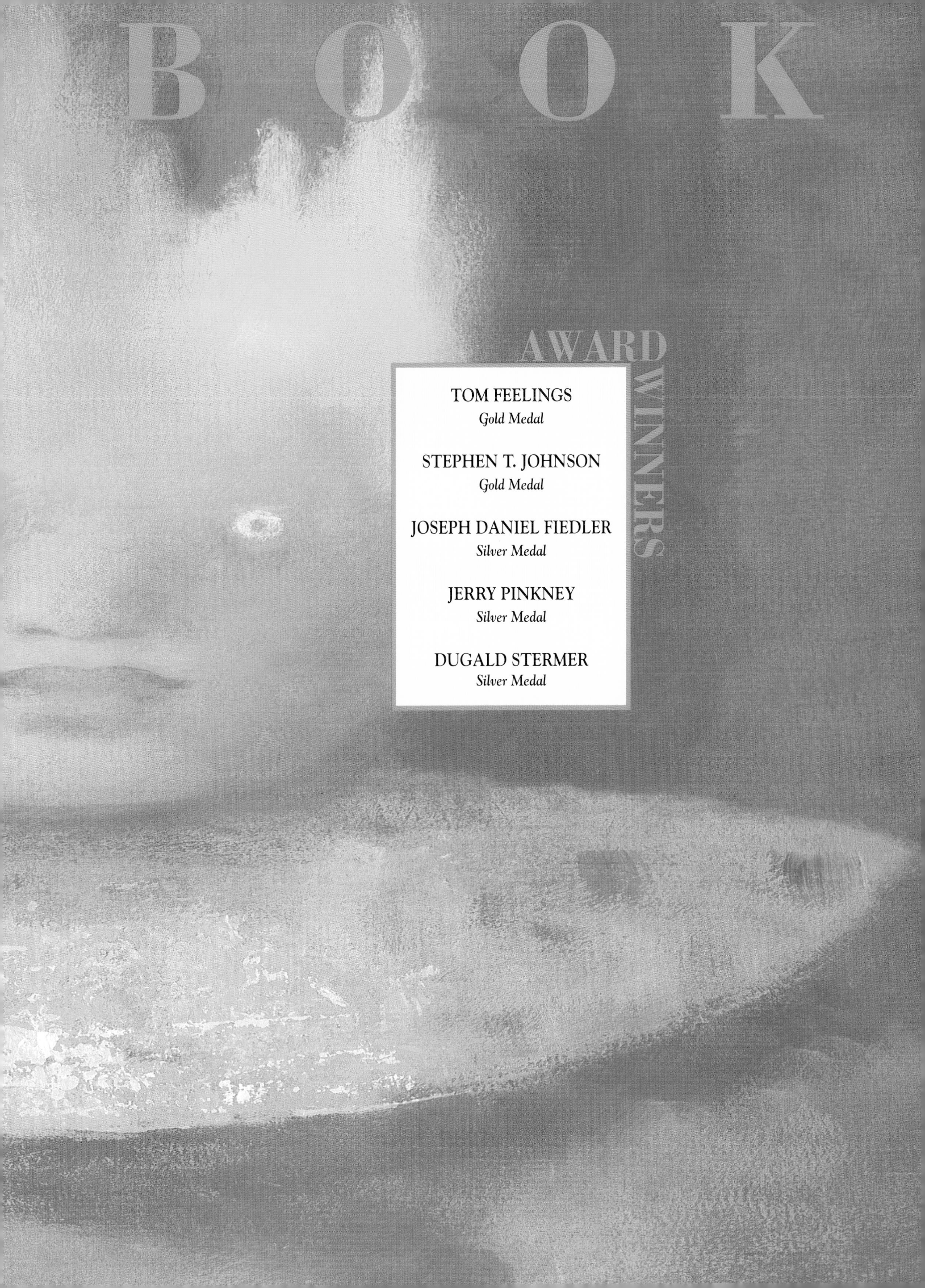

BOOK

AWARD
WINNERS

TOM FEELINGS
Gold Medal

STEPHEN T. JOHNSON
Gold Medal

JOSEPH DANIEL FIEDLER
Silver Medal

JERRY PINKNEY
Silver Medal

DUGALD STERMER
Silver Medal

109

Artist: **TOM FEELINGS**

Art Director: Atha Tehon

Client: Dial Books for Young Readers

Medium: Pen & ink wash on tissue paper

Size: 8" x 19"

Book Gold Medal
TOM FEELINGS

"Throughout the centuries, Africa's powerful celebratory rites have acted as a spiritually strong balancing force to counter the painful experience of slavery. Clearly evident in Black music, Black dance, and athletics— wherever the playing field is level—we innovate, we improvise within the restrictive forms, then transcend them, raising the level of excellence. As a storyteller using the picture form, as an African who was born in America, how could I do anything else but try and live up to that legacy and become a vehicle for this profound, dramatic history to pass through."

109

Artist: **STEPHEN T. JOHNSON**

Art Director: Becky Laughlin

Client: Viking/Penguin

Medium: Pastel, watercolor, gouache, charcoal on paper

Size: 26 ¹/₂" x 22 ¹/₂"

Book Gold Medal
STEPHEN T. JOHNSON

"Since childhood, I have been drawn to the particular energy one senses in people, sounds, and structures, old and new, that constitute a city. The idea for *Alphabet City* came to me while I was walking along a city street. I noticed an ornamental keystone that looked like the letter S. Then suddenly, I saw the letter A in a construction sawhorse and the letter Z in fire escapes. At that moment, it became clear that in urban compositions I could discover the elements that form the letters of the alphabet."

111

Artist: **JOSEPH DANIEL FIEDLER**

Art Director: Alan Dingman

Client: St. Martin's Press

Medium: Alkyd

Size: 14" x 9"

Book Silver Medal

JOSEPH DANIEL FIEDLER

"As an artist, it seems to me that everyone is always talking about talent. I would prefer to think that it is my imagination that is most important. I believe that the ability to imagine things, coupled with an intense curiosity about the world, sustains the persistence to master skills. My maternal grandfather was a sign painter and my paternal grandfather was a skilled woodworker. My father is a natural bricoleur. His brother, my uncle, once invented a device that cut new tread into bald tires so that he could get more mileage out of them. Skills can be learned but imagination comes with the kit."

112

Artist: **JERRY PINKNEY**

Art Director: Barbara Fitzsimmons

Client: Books of Wonder/Morrow

Medium: Pencil, watercolor on Arches

Size: 8 1/2" x 6"

Book Silver Medal

JERRY PINKNEY

"Over the last eight years I have illustrated many of the stories that fascinated me as a child. These stories most likely influenced my interest in visual storytelling, where I now spend most of my creative energy. *The Jungle Book* by Rudyard Kipling is one of those extraordinary tales that helped an inner-city child stretch his imagination. In this portrait of Shere Khan, I tried to show both sides of the animal's character: one of majestic beauty, the other menacing and dark. The jackal, Tabaqui, added a touch of foolishness—sort of like real life, wouldn't you say?"

113

Artist: **DUGALD STERMER**

Art Director: Dugald Stermer

Client: Collins Publishers

Medium: Pencil, watercolor on Arches

Size: 14" x 11"

Book Silver Medal
DUGALD STERMER

"Prior to writing this, I scanned a number of paragraphs by admired colleagues in previous annuals, searching for a model; unsurprisingly, none emerged. So, this piece is one of a series of sixty-some drawings of mammals, birds, reptiles, fish and insects coupling in the act of making offspring, all of which were collected into a book entitled *Birds & Bees* for HarperCollins. For me, the wonderful thing about doing books is that I can exercise my curiosity along with my pencil."

113 B L A C K R H I N O C E R O S

114

114

Artist: **THOM ANG**

Art Director: Rich Thomas

Client: White Wolf Publishing

Medium: Mixed on paper

Size: 12" x 16"

115

Artist: **RACHEL BLISS**

Medium: Oil, acrylic on canvas

Size: 15" x 22"

115

116

Artist: **MICHAEL J. DEAS**

Art Director: Georgia Morrissey

Client: Random House

Medium: Oil on panel

Size: 26" x 16"

117

Artist: **DAVID CHRISTIANA**

Art Director: Michael Farmer

Client: Harcourt Brace & Co./
Jane Yolen Books

Medium: Watercolor on Arches paper

Size: 11" x 8"

118

Artist: **DAVID CHRISTIANA**

Art Director: Diane D'Andrea

Client: Harcourt Brace & Co.

Medium: Watercolor, pencil on paper

Size: 14" x 11"

119

Artist: **ALAN E. COBER**

Art Director: Martha Phillips

Client: Franklin Library/Mint

Medium: Mixed

Size: 8" x 11"

117

118

119

120

Artist: **JODY HEWGILL**

Art Director: Debra Morton Hoyt

Client: W.W. Norton

Medium: Acrylic on board

121

Artist: **MARK GRAHAM**

Art Director: Barbara Fitzsimmons

Client: William Morrow Co.

Medium: Oil on paper

Size: 11" x 17"

122

Artist: **GLENN HARRINGTON**

Art Director: Jim Plumeri

Client: Bantam Doubleday Dell

Medium: Oil on board

Size: 20" x 13"

123

Artist: **JOHN COLLIER**

Art Director: Wendy Bass

Client: Macmillan Publishing Co.

Medium: Pastel

Size: 26" x 16"

121

122

123

124

Artist: **SERGIO MARTINEZ**

Art Director: Jim Plumeri

Client: Bantam Doubleday Dell

Medium: Watercolor, pencil

Size: 12" x 9"

125

Artist: **MICHELLE BARNES**

Medium: Mixed

Size: 16" X 16"

126

Artist: **JERRY PINKNEY**

Art Directors: Nancy Leo
Atha Tehon

Client: Dial Books for Young Readers

Medium: Pencil, watercolor on Arches

Size: 11" x 17"

127

Artist: **BERNIE FUCHS**

Art Director: Atha Tehon

Client: Dial Books for Young Readers

Medium: Oil on canvas

Size: 16" x 36"

124

125

126

127

128

Artist: **RAUL COLON**

Art Director: Chris Hammill Paul

Client: Orchard Books

Medium: Mixed

Size: 14" x 17"

129

Artist: **RAUL COLON**

Art Director: Chris Hammill Paul

Client: Orchard Books

Medium: Mixed

Size: 14" x 17"

130

Artist: **RAUL COLON**

Art Director: Chris Hammill Paul

Client: Orchard Books

Medium: Mixed

Size: 15" x 16"

131

Artist: **BRALDT BRALDS**

Art Director: Steve Snider

Client: Little, Brown & Co.

Medium: Oil on masonite

Size: 15" x 16"

128

129

130

131

132

Artist: **RAFAL OLBINSKI**

Art Director: Rita Marshall

Client: Creative Education

Medium: Acrylic on canvas

Size: 28" x 22"

133

Artist: **DON DAILY**

Art Director: Nancy Loggins Gonzales

Client: Running Press

Medium: Watercolor

Size: 15" x 22"

134

Artist: **GREG COUCH**

Art Director: Lucille Chomowicz

Client: Simon & Schuster

Medium: Colored pencil, acrylic on board

Size: 12" x 9"

135

Artist: **GREG COUCH**

Art Director: Lucille Chomowicz

Client: Simon & Schuster

Medium: Colored pencil, acrylic on board

Size: 12" x 9"

132

133

134

135

136

Artist: **ETIENNE DELESSERT**

Agency: Keiler & Co.

Client: Deloitte & Touche

Medium: Watercolor

Size: 11" x 11"

137

Artist: **S. SAELIG GALLAGHER**

Art Director: Michael Farmer

Client: Harcourt Brace & Co.

Medium: Acrylic

Size: 17" x 15"

138

Artist: **SUZANNE DURANCEAU**

Art Directors: Laura Geringer
Thomas Starace

Client: HarperCollins

Medium: Acrylic, mixed on board

Size: 13" x 9"

139

Artist: **GREG COUCH**

Art Director: Lucille Chomowicz

Client: Simon & Schuster

Medium: Colored pencil, acrylic on board

Size: 12" x 15"

136

137

138

139

140

Artist: **LEONID GORE**

Art Director: David Saylor

Client: Houghton Mifflin Co.

Medium: Acrylic on board

Size: 14" x 12 ¹/₂"

141

Artist: **FRED OTNES**

Art Director: Jim Plumeri

Client: Bantam Doubleday Dell

Medium: Mixed, collage

Size: 30" x 37"

142

Artist: **JAMES GURNEY**

Art Director: Scott Usher

Client: Turner Publishing, Inc.

Medium: Oil on canvas mounted on board

Size: 20" x 57"

143

Artist: **DAVID CHRISTIANA**

Art Director: Phoebe Yeh

Client: Scholastic Inc.

Medium: Watercolor on paper

Size: 11" x 16"

140

141

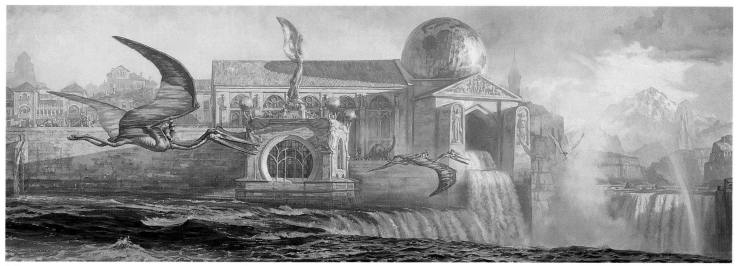

142

143

144

Artist: **DAVID M. BOWERS**

Art Director: Anne Twomey

Client: St. Martin's Press

Medium: Oil on masonite

Size: 18" x 11"

145

Artist: **JOHN JUDE PALENCAR**

Art Director: David Stevenson

Client: Ballantine Books

Medium: Acrylic, mounted Strathmore on 500 plate surface

Size: 14" x 39"

146

Artist: **MERRITT DEKLE**

Art Director: Jackie Merri Meyer

Client: Warner Books

Medium: Acrylic on board

Size: 17" x 11"

147

Artists: **LEO & DIANE DILLON**

Art Director: Elizabeth B. Parisi

Client: Scholastic Inc.

Medium: Mixed

Size: 19" x 14"

145

146

147

148

Artist: **TOM CURRY**

Art Director: Marty Phillips

Client: The Franklin Library

Medium: Acrylic on board

Size: 13" x 9"

149

Artist: **JAMES GURNEY**

Art Director: Scott Usher

Client: Turner Publishing, Inc.

Medium: Oil on board

Size: 12" x 25"

150

Artist: **TOM CURRY**

Art Director: Melanie Kroupa

Client: Orchard Books

Medium: Acrylic on board

Size: 11" x 9"

151

Artist: **TOM CURRY**

Art Director: Melanie Kroupa

Client: Orchard Books

Medium: Acrylic on board

Size: 10" x 9"

148

149

150

151

152

Artist: **JOHN JUDE PALENCAR**

Art Directors: Jerry Todd
George Cornell

Client: Penguin USA

Medium: Watercolor, acrylic, mounted
Strathmore on 500 plate surface

Size: 13" x 14"

153

Artist: **FRED OTNES**

Art Director: Mike Scricco

Client: Deloitte & Touche

Medium: Mixed, wood-collage

Size: 18" x 20"

154

Artist: **MARY GRANDPRÉ**

Art Director: Isabel Warren-Lynch

Client: Random House

Medium: Pastel on paper

Size: 20" x 24"

155

Artist: **RICHARD EGIELSKI**

Art Directors: Laura Geringer
Richard Egielski

Client: Laura Geringer Books

Medium: Watercolor, gouache on paper

Size: 11" x 16"

152

153

154

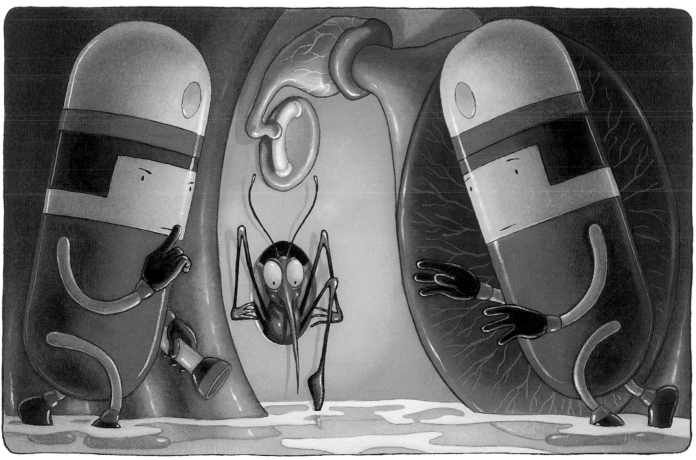

155

156

Artist: **H.B. LEWIS**

Art Director: Leslie Bauman

Client: Troll Communications

Medium: Pastel on paper

Size: 12" x 15"

157

Artist: **TOM FEELINGS**

Art Director: Atha Tehon

Client: Dial Books for Young Readers

Medium: Pen & ink wash on tissue paper

Size: 9 ¼" x 12"

158

Artist: **TOM FEELINGS**

Art Director: Atha Tehon

Client: Dial Books for Young Readers

Medium: Pen & ink wash on tissue paper

Size: 9" x 16"

159

Artist: **TOM FEELINGS**

Art Director: Atha Tehon

Client: Dial Books for Young Readers

Medium: Pen & ink wash on tissue paper

Size: 9" x 20"

156

157

158

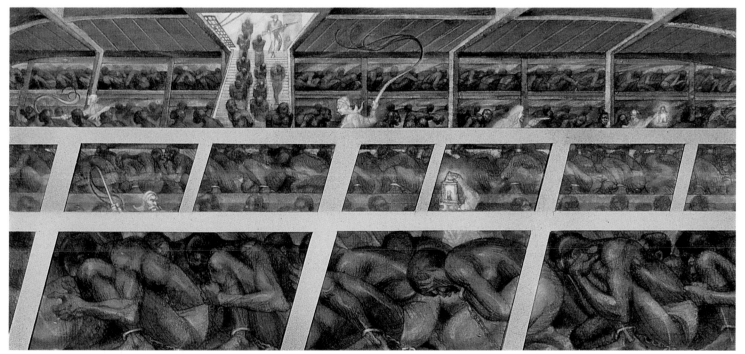

159

160

Artist: **JAMES RANSOME**

Art Director: Golda Laurens

Client: Tambourine Books

Medium: Oil on paper

Size: 15" x 12"

161

Artist: **JAMES RANSOME**

Art Director: Robert Warren

Client: HarperCollins

Medium: Oil on paper

Size: 9" x 10"

162

Artist: **KUNIO HAGIO**

Art Director: Richarda Hellner

Client: Holt Rinehart Winston

Medium: Oil on canvas board

Size: 18" x 24"

163

Artist: **KUNIO HAGIO**

Art Director: Richarda Hellner

Client: Holt Rinehart Winston

Medium: Oil on canvas board

Size: 16" x 20"

160

161

162

163

164

Artist: **CHRISTINE A. FRANCIS**

Client: Four Walls Eight Windows

Medium: Mixed, dimensional

Size: 25 1/2" x 16 1/2"

165

Artists: **STEVE JOHNSON LOU FANCHER**

Art Director: Lou Fancher

Client: Viking/Penguin

Medium: Acrylic on gessoed paper

Size: 13" x 21"

166

Artist: **JERRY PINKNEY**

Art Director: Barbara Fitzsimmons

Client: Books of Wonder/Morrow

Medium: Pencil, watercolor on Arches

Size: 8 1/2" x 6"

167

Artist: **JERRY PINKNEY**

Art Director: Barbara Fitzsimmons

Client: Books of Wonder/Morrow

Medium: Pencil, watercolor on Arches

Size: 9" x 6"

164

165

166

167

168

Artist: **JOHN JUDE PALENCAR**

Art Director: John Fontana

Client: Scribner's

Medium: Acrylic, mounted Strathmore on 500 plate surface

Size: 17" x 17"

169

Artist: **MARK GRAHAM**

Art Director: Barbara Fitzsimmons

Client: William Morrow Co.

Medium: Oil on paper

Size: 11" x 14"

170

Artist: **MATTHEW FREY**

Medium: Oil on gessoed plywood

Size: 21" x 16"

171

Artist: **BERNIE FUCHS**

Art Director: Atha Tehon

Client: Dial Books for Young Readers

Medium: Oil on canvas

Size: 23" x 17"

168

169

170

171

172
Artist: **MARK A. FREDRICKSON**

Art Director: Tom Egner

Client: Avon Books

Medium: Acrylic on board

Size: 17" x 12"

173
Artist: **GREG HARLIN**

Art Director: Paul Buckley

Client: Penguin USA

Medium: Acrylic on board

Size: 9" x 6"

174
Artist: **JORDIN ISIP**

Art Director: Melinda Beck

Client: The New Press

Medium: Mixed

Size: 22 ³/₄" x 15 ³/₈"

175
Artist: **STEPHEN T. JOHNSON**

Art Director: Becky Laughlin

Client: Viking/Penguin

Medium: Pastel, watercolor, gouache,
charcoal on paper

Size: 21" x 35"

172

173

174

175

176

Artist: **DAVE McKEAN**

Art Director: Dave McKean

Client: Vertigo/DC Comics

Medium: Mixed, Mac computer

Size: 10" x 8"

177

Artist: **GARY KELLEY**

Art Director: George Cornell

Client: Viking/Penguin

Medium: Pastel on paper

Size: 24" x 14"

178

Artist: **JOEL PETER JOHNSON**

Art Directors: Elizabeth B. Parisi
Madelina S. Stefan

Client: Scholastic Inc.

Medium: Oil, acrylic on board

Size: 12" x 8"

179

Artist: **JOEL PETER JOHNSON**

Art Director: Victor Weaver

Client: Hyperion

Medium: Oil, acrylic on board

Size: 9" x 7"

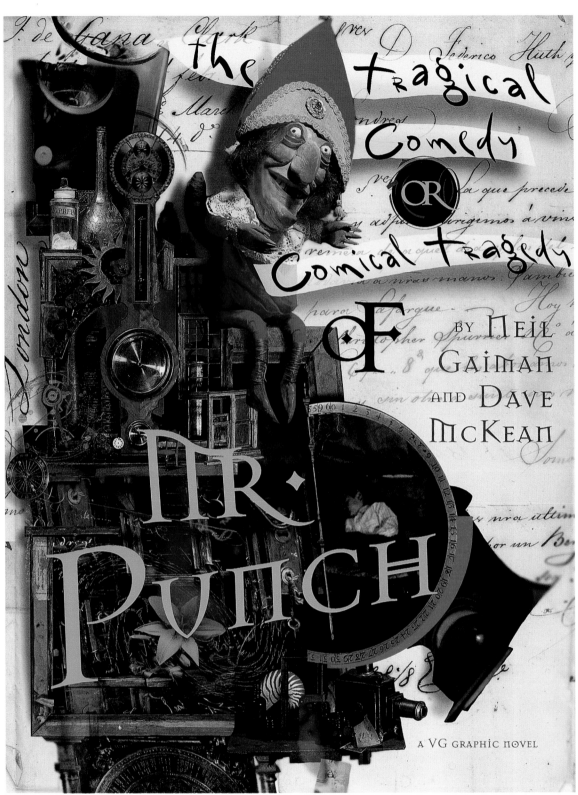

177

178

179

180

Artist: **DAVID SHANNON**

Art Director: Kathleen Westray

Client: Scholastic Inc.

Medium: Acrylic on board

Size: 14" x 13"

181

Artist: **CHRISTOPHER PUGLIESE**

Medium: Oil on wood

Size: 8" x 6"

182

Artist: **JIM La MARCHE**

Client: Harcourt Brace & Co.

Medium: Acrylic washes, colored pencil on
watercolor paper

Size: 11" x 27"

183

Artist: **MAUREEN MEEHAN**

Art Director: Joni Friedman

Client: Putnam Berkley Publishing Group

Medium: Oil, acrylic, graphite on paper

Size: 11 1/2" x 8"

180

181

182

183

184

Artist: **WILLIAM LOW**

Art Director: Leslie Bauman

Client: Bridgewater Books

Medium: Oil on board

Size: 24" x 36"

185

Artist: **WILLIAM LOW**

Art Director: Leslie Bauman

Client: Bridgewater Books

Medium: Oil on board

Size: 24" x 36"

186

Artist: **WILLIAM LOW**

Art Director: Leslie Bauman

Client: Bridgewater Books

Medium: Oil on board

Size: 24" x 36"

187

Artist: **HERB TAUSS**

Art Directors: Ellen Dreyer
Barbara Fitzsimmons

Client: Morrow Junior Books

Medium: Charcoal on canvas

Size: 17" x 27"

184

185

186

187

188

Artist: **EDWARD SOREL**

Art Director: Carol Carson

Client: Alfred A. Knopf

Medium: Watercolor on Bond paper

Size: 14" x 17"

189

Artist: **EDWARD SOREL**

Art Director: Carol Carson

Client: Alfred A. Knopf

Medium: Watercolor on Bond paper

Size: 14" x 17"

190

Artist: **STEPHEN T. JOHNSON**

Art Director: Becky Laughlin

Client: Viking/Penguin

Medium: Pastel, watercolor, gouache, charcoal on paper

Size: 32 ¼" x 22 ½"

191

Artist: **KAM MAK**

Client: Delacorte Press

Medium: Oil on panel

Size: 18" x 11"

188

189

190

191

192

Artist: **MARK SUMMERS**

Art Director: John Kelly

Client: Barnes & Noble, Inc.

Medium: Scratchboard, watercolor

Size: 10" x 8"

193

Artist: **MARK SUMMERS**

Art Director: John Kelly

Client: Barnes & Noble, Inc.

Medium: Scratchboard, watercolor

Size: 12" x 9"

194

Artist: **MARK SUMMERS**

Art Director: John Kelly

Client: Barnes & Noble, Inc.

Medium: Scratchboard, watercolor

Size: 10" x 8"

195

Artist: **DUGALD STERMER**

Art Director: Dugald Stermer

Client: Collins Publisher

Medium: Pencil, watercolor on Arches

Size: 10" x 15"

192

193

194

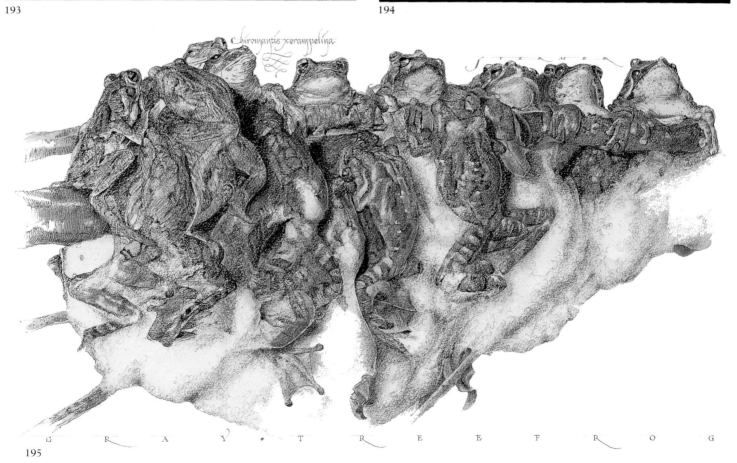

195

196

Artist: **BRAD WEINMAN**

Art Director: Michael Farmer

Client: Harcourt Brace & Co.

Medium: Oil on paper

Size: 16" x 11"

197

Artist: **SALVATORE MURDOCCA**

Art Director: Rachel Simon

Client: Lothrop, Lee & Shepard

Medium: Watercolor, pencil on Arches

Size: 11" x 18"

198

Artist: **BILL KOEB**

Art Director: Joe Pruett

Client: Mad Hatter Studios

Medium: Mixed on Bristol board

Size: 14" x 11"

199

Artist: **ADAM McCAULEY**

Art Director: Toni Ellis

Client: University of Chicago Press

Medium: Mixed on watercolor paper

Size: 9 1/4" x 7"

197

198

199

200

Artist: **DAVID TAMURA**

Art Director: Vaughn Andrews

Client: Harcourt Brace & Co.

Medium: Oil on masonite

Size: 11" x 9"

201

Artist: **DUGALD STERMER**

Art Director: Dugald Stermer

Client: Collins Publishers

Medium: Pencil, watercolor on Arches

Size: 10" x 8"

202

Artist: **WENDELL MINOR**

Art Director: Vaughn Andrews

Client: Harcourt Brace & Co.

Medium: Acrylic on masonite panel

Size: 13" x 9"

203

Artist: **WENDELL MINOR**

Art Director: Vaughn Andrews

Client: Harcourt Brace & Co.

Medium: Acrylic on masonite panel

Size: 19 ¹/₂" x 12"

200

201

202

203

204

Artist: **JOHN THOMPSON**

Art Director: Claire Counihan

Client: Scholastic Inc.

Medium: Acrylic on Strathmore Bristol

Size: 13" x 10"

205

Artist: **GREG NEWBOLD**

Art Directors: Richard Erickson
Pat Bagley

Client: Buckaroo Books

Medium: Acrylic on Bristol

Size: 12" x 20"

206

Artist: **ELLEN THOMPSON**

Art Directors: Ellen Friedman
Joann Hill Lovinski

Client: Hyperion Paperbacks for
Children

Medium: Watercolor on Bristol board

Size: 9" x 7"

207

Artist: **STEPHEN T. JOHNSON**

Art Director: Becky Laughlin

Client: Viking/Penguin

Medium: Pastel, watercolor, gouache,
charcoal on paper

Size: 29" x 22"

204

205

206

207

208

Artist: **CLIFF NIELSEN**

Art Director: Michael Farmer

Client: Harcourt Brace & Co.

Medium: Acrylic on board

Size: 16" x 11"

209

Artist: **CATHLEEN TOELKE**

Art Director: Paul Buckley

Client: Penguin USA

Medium: Gouache on watercolor board

Size: 6 ¹/₂" x 17"

210

Artist: **ROY PENDLETON**

Art Director: Julia Kushnirsky

Client: Warner Books

Medium: Acrylic, oil on cotton duck

Size: 10" x 12"

211

Artist: **JON J. MUTH**

Art Director: Richard Bruning

Client: Vertigo/DC Comics

Medium: Watercolor

Size: 10" x 7"

208

209

210

211

212

Artist: **JOHN THOMPSON**

Art Director: Claire Counihan

Client: Scholastic Inc.

Medium: Acrylic on Strathmore Bristol

Size: 11" x 17"

213

Artist: **JOHN THOMPSON**

Art Director: Claire Counihan

Client: Scholastic Inc.

Medium: Acrylic on Strathmore Bristol

Size: 11" x 17"

214

Artist: **STEVEN POLSON**

Art Director: Nick Krenitsky

Client: HarperCollins

Medium: Oil on linen

Size: 15" x 10"

215

Artist: **JEAN FRANÇOIS PODEVIN**

Art Director: Nick Krenitsky

Client: HarperCollins

Medium: Gouache on board

Size: 16" x 11"

212

213

214

215

216

Artist: **DOUGLAS SMITH**

Art Director: Joel Avirom

Client: HarperCollins

Medium: Scratchboard, watercolor

Size: 14" x 9"

217

Artist: **DAVID SHANNON**

Art Director: Lisa Peters

Client: Harcourt Brace & Co.

Medium: Acrylic on board

Size: 12" x 22"

218

Artist: **DUGALD STERMER**

Art Director: Dugald Stermer

Client: Collins Publishers

Medium: Colored pencils on black
    paper

Size: 10" x 10"

219

Artist: **JAMES NOEL SMITH**

Art Director: Amy Quinlivan

Client: Friend & Johnson, Inc.

Medium: Watercolor

Size: 12" x 9"

The Vanity Burns

217

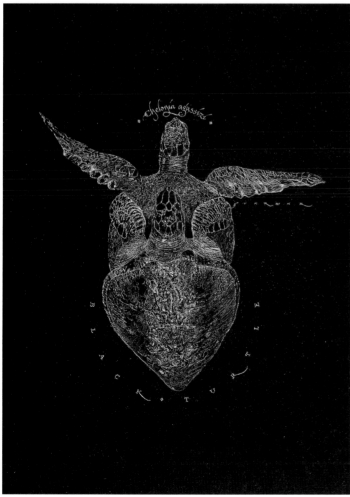

218

219

220

Artist: **PHILLIP A. SINGER**

Art Director: Julia Kushnirsky

Client: Warner Books

Medium: Oil on board

Size: 12" x 9"

221

Artist: **PHILLIP A. SINGER**

Art Director: Diane Luger

Client: Warner Books

Medium: Oil on board

Size: 10" x 7"

222

Artist: **JAMES McMULLAN**

Art Director: Ava Weiss

Client: Greenwillow Books

Medium: Gouache on paper

Size: 8" x 6"

223

Artist: **CASEY CRAIG**

Medium: Torn paper collage on board

Size: 8" x 11"

220

221

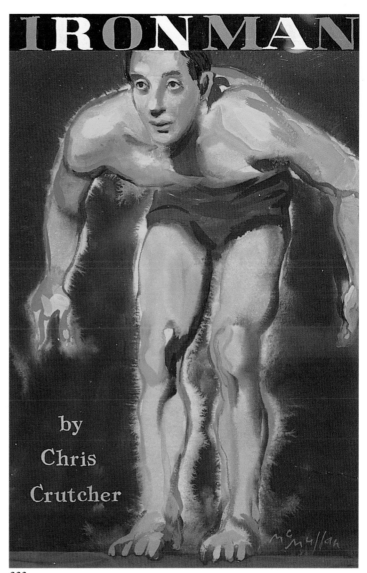

222

223

224

Artist: **GENNADY SPIRIN**

Art Director: Michael Farmer

Client: Harcourt Brace & Co.

225

Artist: **GENNADY SPIRIN**

Art Director: Michael Farmer

Client: Harcourt Brace & Co.

Medium: Watercolor on board

Size: 13" x 18"

226

Artist: **DAVID SHANNON**

Art Director: Elizabeth B. Parisi

Client: Scholastic Inc.

Medium: Acrylic on board

Size: 18" x 14"

227

Artist: **JAMES RANSOME**

Art Director: Golda Laurens

Client: Tambourine Books

Medium: Oil on paper

Size: 15" x 12"

224

ANTON CHEKHOV

Kashtanka

Illustrated by
GENNADY SPIRIN

225

226

227

228

Artist: **KINUKO Y. CRAFT**

Art Director: Paolo Pepe

Client: Simon & Schuster

Medium: Mixed

Size: 15" x 14"

229

Artist: **MURRAY TINKELMAN**

Art Director: Murray Tinkelman

Client: Harcourt Brace & Co.

Medium: Pen & ink on Bristol

Size: 12" x 12"

230

Artist: **MARK ENGLISH**

Art Director: Tim Trabon

Medium: Oil, pastel on canvas

Size: 24" x 36"

231

Artist: **ROBERT FLORCZAK**

Art Director: Michael Farmer

Client: Harcourt Brace & Co.

Medium: Oil on canvas

Size: 32" x 24"

228

229

230

231

ADVERTISING JURY

DIANE DILLON
CHAIRMAN
Illustrator

YVONNE BUCHANAN
Illustrator

CHRISTINE CORNELL
Court Artist

STAVROS COSMOPULOS
President
The Cosmopulos Group

ROB DAY
Illustrator

ARTHUR HOCHSTEIN
Art Director
Time magazine

GARY KELLEY
Illustrator/Educator/Art Director/Designer

GENE LIGHT
Art Director

FRED OTNES
Illustrator

ADVERTISING

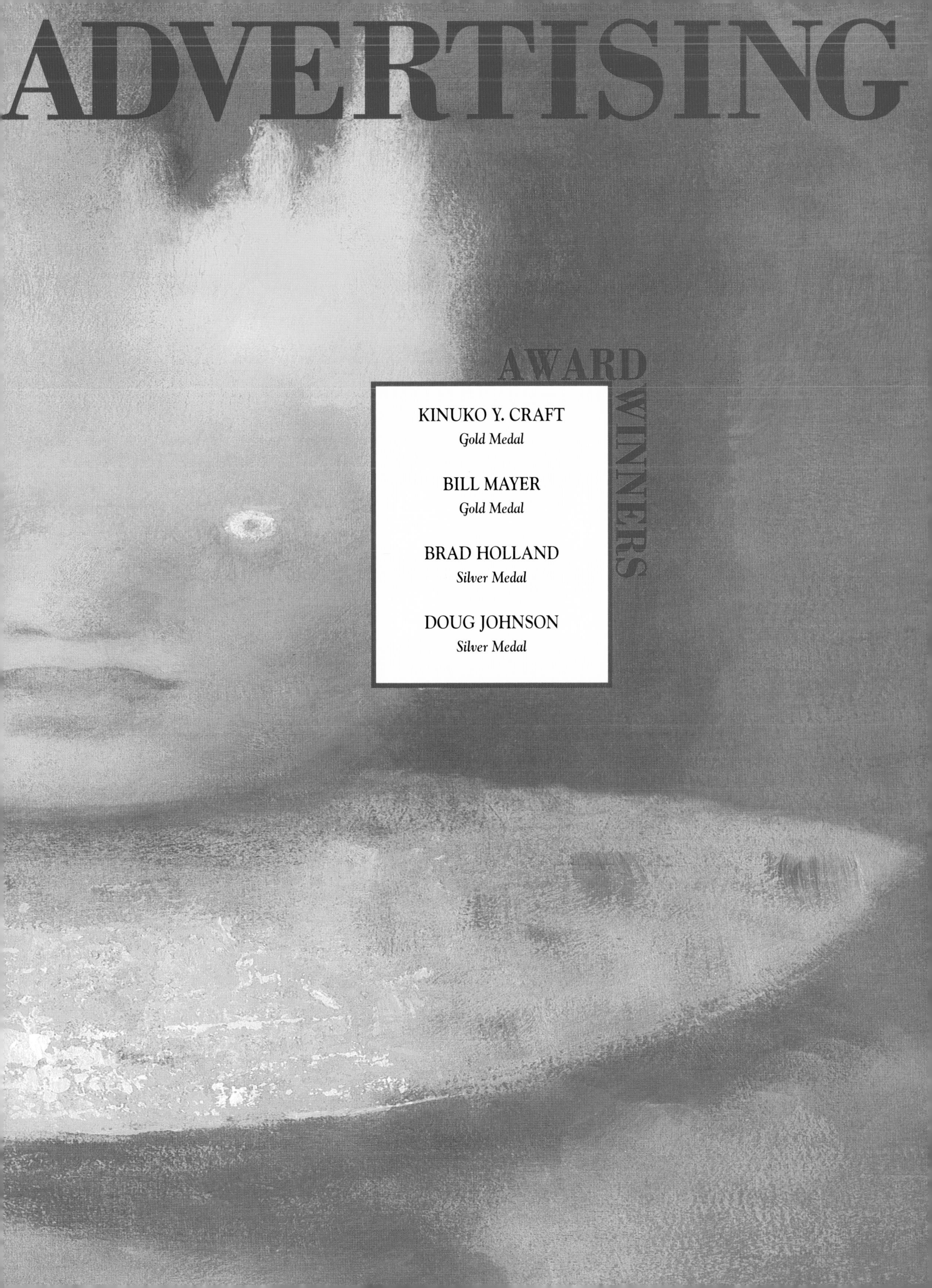

KINUKO Y. CRAFT
Gold Medal

BILL MAYER
Gold Medal

BRAD HOLLAND
Silver Medal

DOUG JOHNSON
Silver Medal

232

Artist: **KINUKO Y. CRAFT**

Art Directors: Collene Currie
Clay Freeman

Client: The Dallas Opera

Medium: Oil, watercolor on board

Size: 22" x 22"

Advertising Gold Medal
KINUKO Y. CRAFT

Kinuko Craft has a three-year contract with the Dallas Opera to create the image for their annual poster. She relies on the music of "Madame Butterfly" itself to clear her thoughts for the task before her. She says it allows her to get deeply into the subject and let the ideas flow forth. Five sketches were requested by the design firm of May and Company. They all received careful consideration by the Dallas Opera's head designer, but those discussions were taxing. "I work best when I've taken a long deadline and waited until the Art Director begins bugging me for the finish." The portrait is not of the actual diva, but Kinuko's own imaginative interpretation of Puccini's narrative.

233

Artist: **BILL MAYER**

Art Directors: Bill Meyer
Jerry Sullivan

Client: Sullivan Haas Coyle

Medium: Airbrush, gouache, dyes on
Strathmore

Size: 16" x 14"

Advertising Gold Medal
BILL MAYER

The artist had to chuckle when he recalled the on again—off again life of this beast. Originally he was asked to create a brochure for the Ohio-based design firm of SBC Advertising. Several animals symbolized the firm's attributes: speedy cheetah, tenacious pit bull, etc. The client felt it needed a happier image. Even a second version failed and the project was off. Months later, Sullivan Haas and Coyle, another client, asked to use the image for their promo poster—on again! The punch line read: "If you have a marketing problem staring you in the face...call us." The menacing menagerie had found a home.

234

Artist: **BRAD HOLLAND**

Art Director: Gary Holme

Agency: Chiat Day

Client: Microsoft Word

Medium: Acrylic on masonite

Size: 19" x 26"

Advertising Silver Medal
BRAD HOLLAND

Chiat Day called me to do a picture of a carnival. I had a lot of ideas laying around other clients had rejected. So I proposed a carnival of rejected ideas. I hope all the clients who turned these ideas down the first time see this and learn their lesson.

235

Artist: **DOUG JOHNSON**

Art Director: Doug Johnson

Client: Dodger Productions/
The Almeida Theatre Co.

Medium: Gouache on board

Size: 23" x 14 1/2"

Advertising Silver Medal
DOUG JOHNSON

Canadian born Doug Johnson and his wife, producer Valerie Gordon-Johnson, devide their time between a loft in Manhattam and a Wyoming ranch. He is a founding partner in Dodger Productions--Winner of 34 "Tony" awards in the last ten years. This poster for the Dodgers/Almeida production of "Hamlet" captures the "lurid" aspects of turn-of-the-century theatre advertisements, while being faithful to the modernity of this "classic," and accurate in the depiction of its leading actor. The hand-lettering was more time consuming and much less fun than the illustration. The only "approved" photo was a soft-focus head shot of star Ralph Fiennes, so Valerie's hands are shown holding a borrowed stage prop skull.

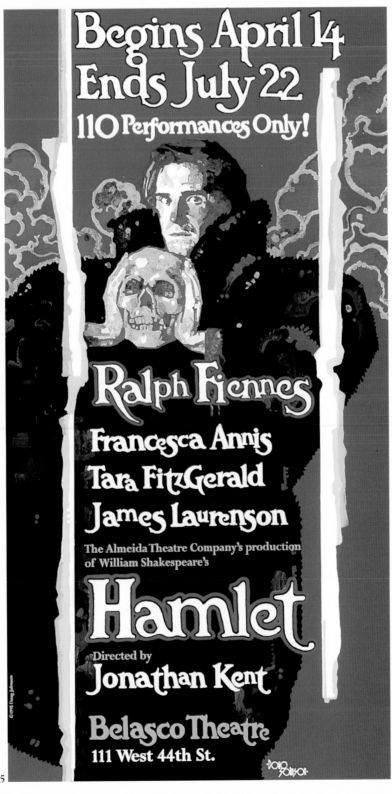

236

Artist: **MELINDA BECK**

Medium: Mixed on board

Size: 17" x 17"

237

Artist: **MELINDA BECK**

Art Director: Satoru Igarashi

Client: Island Records

Medium: Mixed

Size: 13" x 16 1/2"

238

Artist: **GREG CALL**

Art Director: Suwin Chan

Client: Tony Lama

Medium: Oil on board

Size: 22 1/2" x 12"

239

Artist: **STEVEN ADLER**

Art Director: David Shiedt

Agency: Thomas & Perkins

Client: Central City Opera Co.

Medium: Oil on gessoed paper

Size: 22" x 9"

236

237

238

239

240

Artist: **RICHARD COWDREY**

Art Director: Marla Henley

Client: MeadCorp.

Medium: Acrylic on board

Size: 17" x 17"

241

Artist: **JARRETT HAGY**

Art Director: Jarrett Hagy

Client: Indianapolis Indians

Medium: Oil on paper Co.

Size: 7 1/2" x 22 1/2"

242

Artist: **BARBARA BANTHIEN**

Art Director: Lisa Hoffman

Client: Simpson Paper Co.

Medium: Watercolor, pencil on rag
Bristol board

Size: 12 1/2" x 8"

243

Artist: **JAMES R. BENNETT**

Art Director: David Stephenson

Agency: McCann Erickson

Client: Coca-Cola

Medium: Oil on board

Size: 17" x 10"

240

241

242

243

244

Artist: **PETER BOLLINGER**

Client: Concepts

Medium: Silicon Graphic Image/
    Iris print

Size: 15 ¹/2" x 20"

245

Artist: **BUA**

Art Director: Lee Hammond

Client: BMG Music

Medium: Acrylic

Size: 12" x 11 ¹/2"

246

Artist: **PETER BOLLINGER**

Art Director: Doug Michaels

Client: Bluestar Inc.

Medium: Silicon Graphic Image/Iris print

Size: 13" x 10"

247

Artist: **MARK ENGLISH**

Art Director: Tim Trabon

Client: Trabon Paris Printing

Medium: Mixed on paper

Size: 17" x 14"

244

245

246

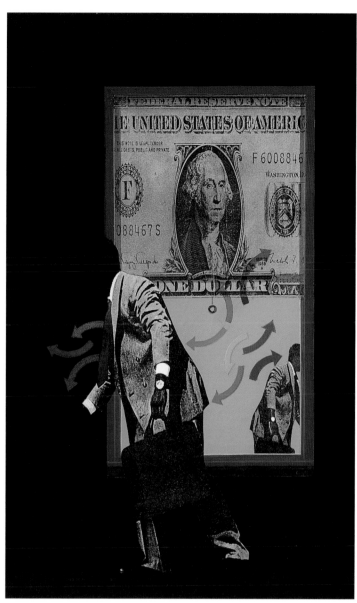

247

248

Artist: **JIM EFFLER**

Art Director: Joseph Stryker

Agency: Northlich Stolley Lawarre

Client: Beckett Paper

Medium: Acrylic

Size: 23 1/2" x 16 1/2"

249

Artist: **ROBERT GIUSTI**

Art Director: Peter Clercx

Agency: J. Walter Thompson Intl.

Client: BMW

Medium: Acrylic on linen

Size: 11 1/2" x 19 1/2"

250

Artist: **ROY CARRUTHERS**

Art Director: Kin Yuen

Client: Time Warner

Medium: Oil on canvas

Size: 12" x 12"

251

Artist: **ROY CARRUTHERS**

Art Director: Joe Ivey

Client: Ciba Geigy

Medium: Oil on canvas

Size: 19" x 16 1/2"

249

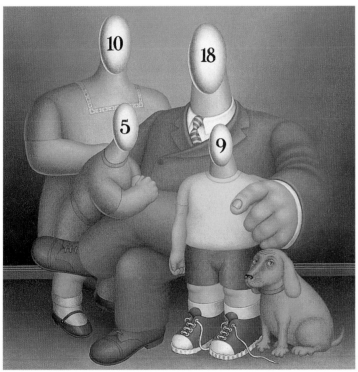

250

251

252

Artist: **SUZANNE DURANCEAU**

Art Director: Suzanne Côté

Agency: Goodhue & Assoc.

Client: Les Epiciers Unis
Metro-Richelieu

Medium: Acrylic, watercolor on board

Size: 14 1/2" x 10"

253

Artist: **BOB CONGE**

Art Director: Lynn Wood

Client: Public Service of New Hampshire

Medium: Pen & ink, watercolor
on Arches

Size: 9 1/2" x 27"

254

Artist: **MARK CHICKINELLI**

Art Director: Karen Sylvia

Client: Union Pacific Railroad

Medium: Oil on canvas board

Size: 27" x 19"

255

Artist: **TOM CURRY**

Art Director: Susan Overstreet

Client: South Coast Repertory Theatre

Medium: Acrylic on board

Size: 12" x 9"

252

253

254

255

256

Artist: **MARK A. FREDRICKSON**

Art Director: Don Anderson

Agency: Jefferson Acker

Client: Sherwood

Medium: Acrylic

Size: 16 ½" x 14 ½"

257

Artist: **MARK A. FREDRICKSON**

Art Director: Don Anderson

Agency: Jefferson Acker

Client: Sherwood

Medium: Acrylic

Size: 13 ½" x 12 ½"

258

Artist: **RHONDA NASS**

Art Director: Susan Casey

Client: Willis & Geiger

Medium: Graphite, acrylic on Bristol board

Size: 12 ½" x 21 ½"

259

Artist: **RHONDA NASS**

Art Director: Susan Casey

Client: Willis & Geiger

Medium: Graphite, acrylic on Bristol board

Size: 12" x 21 ½"

256

257

258

259

260

Artist: **JOE CIARDIELLO**

Art Directors: Tommy Steele
John O'Brien

Client: Capitol Records, Inc.

Medium: Pen & ink, watercolor on paper

Size: 13" x 11"

261

Artist: **JOE CIARDIELLO**

Art Directors: Tommy Steele
John O'Brien

Agency: Capitol Records, Inc.

Client: Capitol Records, Inc.

Medium: Pen & ink, watercolor on paper

Size: 11" x 10"

262

Artist: **NORA KÖERBER**

Art Director: Ricki Poulos

Client: Naras

Medium: Acrylic

Size: 11 1/2" x 8"

263

Artist: **ADAM NIKLEWICZ**

Art Director: Diane Woolverton

Client: U.S. Information Agency

Medium: Acrylic on board

Size: 15 1/2" x 10"

260 Roy Brown

261 T-Bone Walker

262

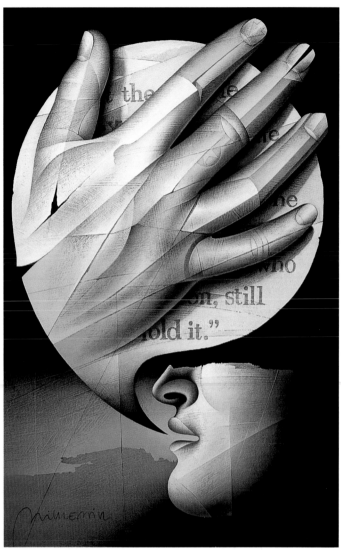

263

264

Artist: **KEITH GRAVES**

Art Director: Lisa Kirkpatrick

Client: Texas Monthly

Medium: Prismacolor, acrylic on board

Size: 14" x 14"

265

Artist: **KEITH GRAVES**

Art Director: Michael Bays

Client: Polygram Records, Inc.

Medium: Prismacolor, acrylic on board

Size: 10" x 10"

266

Artist: **TIM O'BRIEN**

Art Director: Mark Driscoll

Agency: Bates Worldwide

Client: Cunard

Medium: Oil on board

Size: 15" x 9"

267

Artist: **JOHN RUSH**

Art Director: William Hollingshead

Client: Questar Video Inc.

Medium: Oil on masonite

Size: 23 ¹/₂" x 13"

264

265

266

267

268

Artist: **TIM GABOR**

Art Director: Tim Gabor

Client: Roswell Records, Inc.

Medium: Prismacolor on Strathmore

Size: 17" x 14"

269

Artist: **JOEL NAKAMURA**

Art Director: Satoru Igarashi

Client: Island Records

Medium: Mixed on tin

Size: 14" x 14"

270

Artist: **CLARE TAGLIANETTI**

Art Directors: Jacqueline Bofinger
David Savinar

Agency: Devon Direct

Client: Bell Atlantic

Medium: Gouache on board

Size: 8" x 5"

271

Artist: **TIM JESSELL**

Art Director: Sam Beeson

Agency: Fellers & Co.

Client: Hughes Christensen

Medium: Mixed on paper

Size: 15" x 9"

268

269

270

271

272

Artist: **TERESA FASOLINO**

Art Director: Simon Dear

Client: Green Acres Farm

Medium: Oil on canvas

Size: 16" x 10 ¹/₂"

273

Artist: **ROBERT HUNT**

Art Directors: Dave Carson
Clint Golman

Client: Industrial Light & Magic

Medium: Oil on board

Size: 32" x 43"

274

Artist: **GERRY GERSTEN**

Art Directors: Gregor Seitz
Uwe Marquardt

Agency: Ogilvy & Mather

Client: American Express

Medium: Pencil on vellum

Size: 17" x 14"

275

Artist: **MARVIN MATTELSON**

Art Director: Jay Barbieri

Client: Angel EMI Virgin Classics

Medium: Oil on ragboard

Size: 8" x 8"

273

274

275

276

Artist: **BERNIE FUCHS**

Art Director: John Snow

Client: PGA Tour Tournament
Services

Medium: Oil on canvas

Size: 40" x 30"

277

Artist: **JOHN ENGLISH**

Art Director: Carter Weitz

Agency: Bailey Laverman & Assoc.

Client: Western Paper Co.

Medium: Mixed on board

Size: 30" x 20"

278

Artist: **ROB DAY**

Art Director: Bonnie Caldwell

Client: Sybase

Medium: Oil on paper

Size: 14 1/2" x 10 1/2"

279

Artist: **DAVE La FLEUR**

Art Director: Steve Utley

Agency: Quill Creative

Client: Switchview Telecom

Medium: Oil on linen

Size: 10" x 23 1/2"

277

278

279

280

Artist: **GREGORY MANCHESS**

Art Director: Lisa Quon

Client: Patagonia

Medium: Oil on gessoed board

Size: 10 1/2" x 11"

281

Artist: **JORDIN ISIP**

Client: Castle Von Buhler

Medium: Mixed on paper

Size: 22" x 23"

282

Artist: **RAFAL OLBINSKI**

Art Director: Tony Tonkin

Client: Linn Hi-Fi

Medium: Acrylic on canvas

Size: 20 1/2" x 30 1/2"

283

Artist: **RAFAL OLBINSKI**

Art Directors: Ann Murphy
           Jane Oye

Client: New York City Opera

Medium: Acrylic on canvas

Size: 18" x 24"

280

281

282

283

284

Artist: **LINDA DeVITO SOLTIS**

Art Director: Linda DeVito Soltis

Client: Glitterwrap, Inc.

Medium: Acrylic on canvas

Size: 12 1/2" x 14"

285

Artist: **CHRISTIAN NORTHEAST**

Art Director: Jason Gaboriau

Agency: Goldsmith/Jeffrey

Client: Robin Hood Foundation

Medium: Oil, acrylic, paper on wood

286

Artist: **BILL MAYER**

Art Director: John Lionti

Client: Cleveland Film Festival

Medium: Airbrush, gouache, dyes on Strathmore

Size: 17" x 13"

287

Artist: **BILL MAYER**

Medium: Gouache, stamps

Size: 7" x 4 1/2"

284

285

286

287

288

Artist: **JACK N. UNRUH**

Art Director: Grant Richards

Client: Pacific Bell

Medium: Ink, watercolor on board

Size: 15" x 12 ½"

289

Artist: **ETIENNE DELESSERT**

Art Director: Rita Marshall

Client: Creative Co.

Medium: Watercolor

Size: 12" x 9"

290

Artist: **TODD L.W. DONEY**

Art Director: David Golden

Client: DuPont Pharmaceuticals

Medium: Oil on canvas

Size: 23 ½" x 18 ½"

291

Artist: **BART FORBES**

Art Director: Tom Smith

Client: Legends of the Game Museum

Medium: Oil on canvas

Size: 21 ½" x 35 ½"

289

290

291

292

Artist: **MARK A. FREDRICKSON**

Art Director: Marna Henley

Client: Mead Corp.

Medium: Acrylic

Size: 29" x 23"

293

Artist: **BERNIE FUCHS**

Art Director: Lee Mauer

Client: Kohler Co.

Medium: Oil on canvas

Size: 20" x 30"

294

Artist: **BRAD LETHABY**

Art Director: Brad Lethaby

Client: Lake Erie Ballet

Medium: Oil on canvas

Size: 13 ¹/₃" x 26 ¹/₂"

295

Artist: **HODGES SOILEAU**

Client: Ed Acuna

Medium: Oil on canvas

Size: 11" x 9"

292

293

294

295

296

Artist: **JERRY LoFARO**

Art Director: Penny Duerr

Agency: Carmichael Lynch

Client: Cargill Foods

Medium: Acrylic on board

Size: 12 1/2 x 14 1/2"

297

Artist: **BRAD HOLLAND**

Art Director: Jim McClune

Client: Mind Power

Medium: Oil on board

Size: 7" x 10"

298

Artist: **MARCO VENTURA**

Art Director: Roberto Battaglia

Agency: Saatchi & Saatchi

Client: Antinori

Medium: Oil on wood

Size: 6" x 6"

299

Artist: **DEAN PAPPALARDO**

Art Director: Dean Pappalardo

Client: Road Runner Records

Medium: Computer generated, clay

Size: 5" x 5"

296

297

298

299

300

Artist: **SALLY WERN COMPORT**

Art Director: Kurt D.L. Dietsch

Client: North Park College

Medium: Dyes, pastels, charcoal on pastel cloth

Size: 12" x 15"

301

Artist: **ERIC WHITE**

Art Director: Eric White

Client: Dr. Strange Records

Medium: Acrylic, collage on Bristol

Size: 12" x 12"

302

Artist: **JOHN H. HOWARD**

Art Director: Harriet Winner

Client: Booz Allen & Hamilton

Medium: Acrylic on canvas

Size: 24" x 36"

303

Artist: **GENE SPARKMAN**

Art Director: Tom Geary

Client: The Geary Gallery

Medium: Pastel on paper

Size: 20" x 29"

300

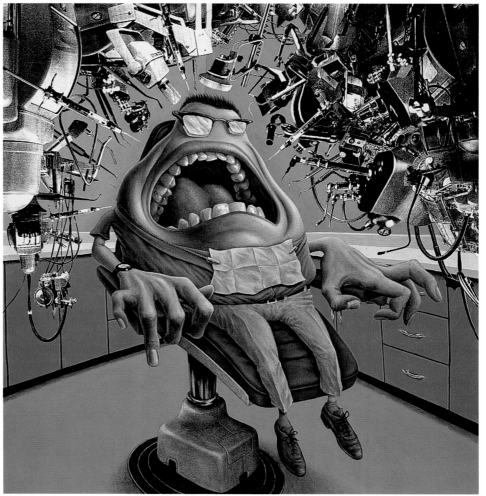

301

302

303

304

Artist: **DON WELLER**

Art Director: Don Weller

Client: Gastronomy

Medium: Ink overlay, colored pencil on plastic over paper

Size: 13 1/2" x 12"

305

Artist: **BRALDT BRALDS**

Art Director: Dyang Phorruh

Client: Delta Airlines International

Medium: Oil on masonite

Size: 20 1/2" x 18"

306

Artists: **BERNARD UY
JAMES NESBITT**

Art Directors: Bernard Uy
James Nesbitt

Client: Kiva Han Cafe

Medium: Mixed, digital

Size: 6 1/2" x 5"

307

Artist: **WIKTOR SADOWSKI**

Art Director: Susan Overstreet

Client: South Coast Repertory Theatre

Medium: Acrylic

Size: 17 1/2" x 12 1/2"

304

305

306

307

308

Artist: **BILL JAMES**

Medium: Pastel on board

Size: 35" x 26"

309

Artist: **DAVE La FLEUR**

Art Director: Tim Bade

Agency: The Marlin Co.

Client: Reckitt & Colman
Commercial Group

Medium: Oil on linen

Size: 16 ½" x 12"

310

Artist: **DAVE La FLEUR**

Art Director: Tim Bade

Agency: The Marlin Co.

Client: Reckitt & Colman
Commercial Group

Medium: Oil on linen

Size: 16 ½" x 12"

311

Artist: **MICHAEL SCANLAN**

Art Director: John Nagy

Client: Sive Young Rubicam

Medium: Pencil, gesso on board

Size: 9" x 12"

308

309

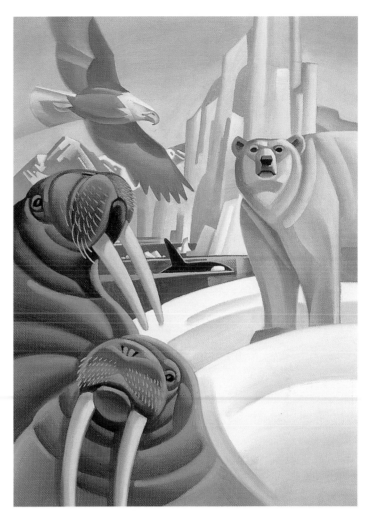

310

311

312

Artist: **FRANCIS LIVINGSTON**

Art Director: Terry Pimsleur

Client: Terry Pimsleur & Co., Inc.

Medium: Oil on board

Size: 21" x 15"

313

Artist: **LUBA LUKOVA**

Client: The Living Theatre

Medium: Mixed on board

Size: 23" x 18"

314

Artist: **LUBA LUKOVA**

Client: The Living Theatre

Medium: Mixed on board

Size: 23" x 18"

315

Artist: **BILL MAYER**

Art Director: Beth Rokicki

Agency: Foote Cone & Belding

Client: Levi's Jeans for Women

Medium: Ink

Size: 9 1/2" x 14"

313

314

315

316

Artist: **ALAN WITSCHONKE**

Art Director: Lilla Rogers

Medium: Collage, oil on masonite

Size: 15 1/2" x 12 1/2"

317

Artist: **DAVID SHANNON**

Art Director: Susan Overstreet

Client: South Coast Repertory
Theatre

Medium: Acrylic, Prismacolor on
board

Size: 10 1/2" x 7"

318

Artist: **ADAM McCAULEY**

Art Director: Adam McCauley

Client: Great American Music Hall

Medium: Scratchboard, overlay

Size: 16 1/2" x 10"

319

Artist: **WARREN LINN**

Art Director: Stephen Byram

Client: JMT Productions

Medium: Collage, acrylic on plywood

Size: 23 1/2" x 33 1/2"

316

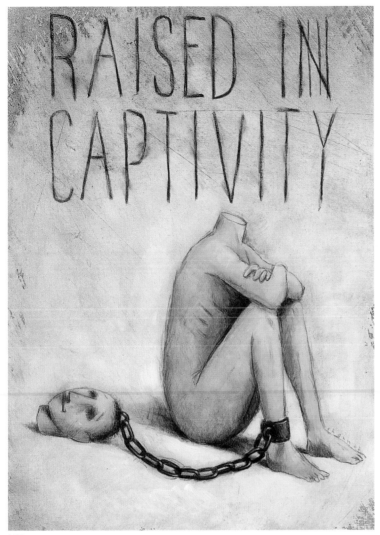

317

318

319

320

Artist: **MARK RIEDY**

Art Director: Jeff Potter

Agency: Foote Cone & Belding

Client: Van Kampen American Capital

Medium: Acrylic on board

Size: 18" x 19"

321

Artist: **PHILIPPE WEISBECKER**

Art Director: Michael Mabry

Client: Deepa Textiles

Medium: Mixed

Size: 9" x 12 ¹/₂"

322

Artist: **RAFAL OLBINSKI**

Art Director: Susan Overstreet

Client: South Coast Repertory Theatre

Medium: Acrylic on canvas

Size: 30" x 20"

323

Artist: **WILL NELSON**

Art Director: Bernie Vangrin

Agency: J. Walter Thompson

Client: Chevron Corp.

Medium: Watercolor, gouache on Strathmore

Size: 17" x 12 ¹/₂"

320

321

322

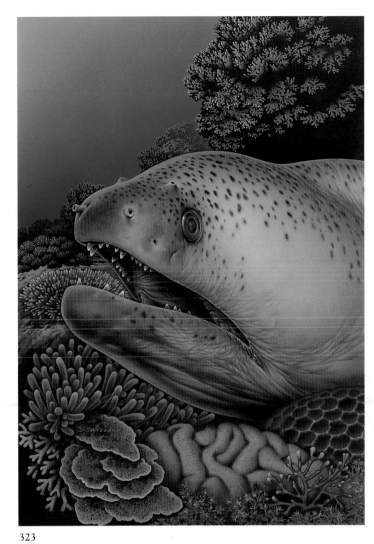

323

324

Artist: **LINDA DeVITO SOLTIS**

Art Director: Linda DeVito Soltis

Client: Glitterwrap, Inc.

Medium: Acrylic on canvas

Size: 15" x 12"

325

Artist: **JAMES GORDON MEEK**

Art Director: John Martin Meek

Client: HMI, Inc. Communications

Medium: Scratchboard

Size: 19" x 12 1/2"

326

Artist: **SCOTT MACK**

Medium: Oil on board

Size: 7 1/2" x 5 1/2"

327

Artist: **BRUCE WOLFE**

Client: Mendocino Music Festival
Assoc.

Medium: Oil on canvas

Size: 24" x 36"

324

325

326

327

328

Artist: **GRETCHEN DOW
SIMPSON**

Art Director: Pamela Kuehl

Client: Winross

Medium: Oil on panel

Size: 8 ¹/₂" x 12 ¹/₂"

329

Artist: **PHILIPPE WEISBECKER**

Art Director: Greg Galvan

Client: Resource Net International

Medium: Mixed, collage

Size: 17 ¹/₂" x 23 ¹/₂"

330

Artist: **MARK ENGLISH**

Art Director: Tim Trabon

Client: Trabon Paris Printing

Medium: Mixed on paper

Size: 17" x 12"

331

Artist: **ED LINDLOF**

Art Director: Kit Hinrichs

Client: Simpson Paper Co.

Medium: Acrylic, inks on cotton
Bristol

Size: 22" x 14"

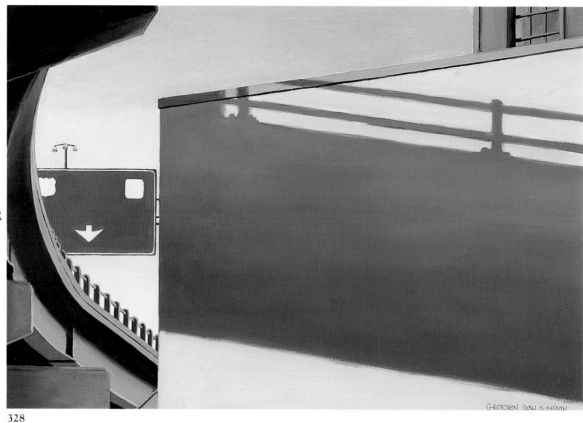

328

329

330

331

332

Artist: **DANIEL SCHWARTZ**

Art Director: Gail Sanfilippo

Agency: Ogilvy & Mather

Client: Microsoft

Medium: Oil on canvas

Size: 20" x 17"

333

Artist: **MARVIN MATTELSON**

Art Director: Kyle Grazia

Agency: Sandler Communications

Client: Burroughs Wellcome

Medium: Oil on ragboard

Size: 7 1/2" x 10"

334

Artist: **LAMONT O'NEAL**

Medium: Gouache

Size: 13 1/2" x 10 1/2"

335

Artist: **KEITH GRAVES**

Art Director: Lisa Kirkpatrick

Client: Texas Monthly

Medium: Prismacolor, acrylic on board

Size: 18 1/2" x 13 1/2"

332

333

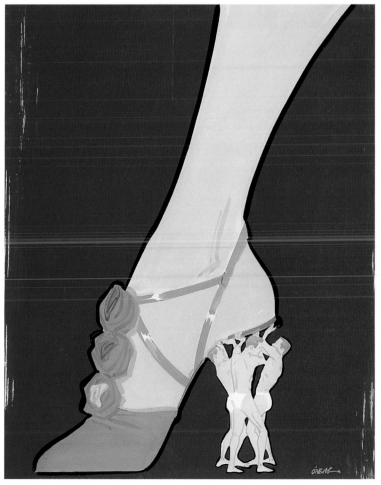

334

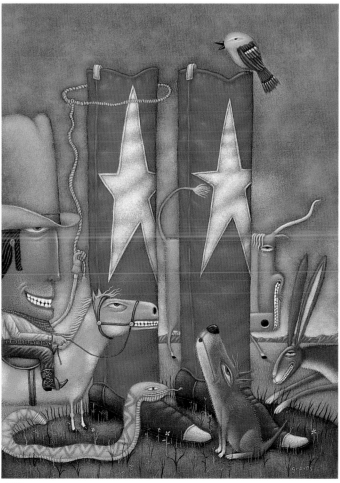

335

336

Artist: **DAVID M. BOWERS**

Art Director: David Whitmore

Client: TLC Monthly

Medium: Oil on masonite

Size: 14 ¼" x 10"

337

Artist: **GUY PORFIRIO**

Art Director: John Rafferty

Client: J. D'Addario & Co.

Medium: Watercolor, pencil on board

Size: 28" x 23"

338

Artist: **GREGORY MANCHESS**

Art Director: Jay Johnson

Client: Colorado Cyclist

Medium: Oil on gessoed board

Size: 19" x 14 ½"

339

Artist: **MARVIN MATTELSON**

Art Director: Steve Ohman

Client: Lowe & Partners

Medium: Oil on ragboard

Size: 8" x 6"

336

337

338

339

340

Artist: **POLLY BECKER**

Art Director: Fritz Klaetke

Client: Division Street

Medium: Mixed

Size: 15 ¹/₂" X 11"

341

Artist: **BRALDT BRALDS**

Art Director: Jerry Sears

Client: St. Louis Zoo/Purina Mills

Medium: Oil on masonite

Size: 22" x 26"

342

Artist: **YVONNE BUCHANAN**

Art Director: Michael Hammond

Agency: Ogilvy & Mather

Client: American Express

Medium: Pen & ink

Size: 13 ¹/₂" x 10 ¹/₂"

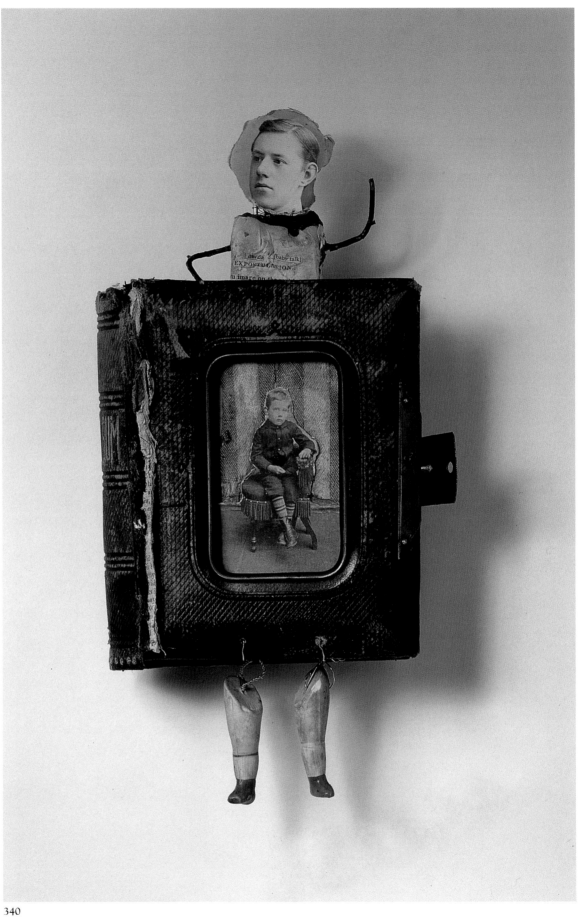

340

341

342

INSTITUTIONAL JURY

JOHN THOMPSON
CHAIRMAN
Illustrator/Professor, Syracuse University

BRIAN AJHAR
Illustrator

CARTER GOODRICH
Illustrator

EDMUND GUY
Illustrator

JOHN MAGGARD III
Illustrator

GENE MYDLOWSKI
V.P. Creative Director
Harper Paperbacks

NANCY STAHL
Illustrator

ANNE TWOMEY
Art Director
St. Martin's Press

FRED WOODWARD
Art Director
Rolling Stone

INSTITUTIONAL

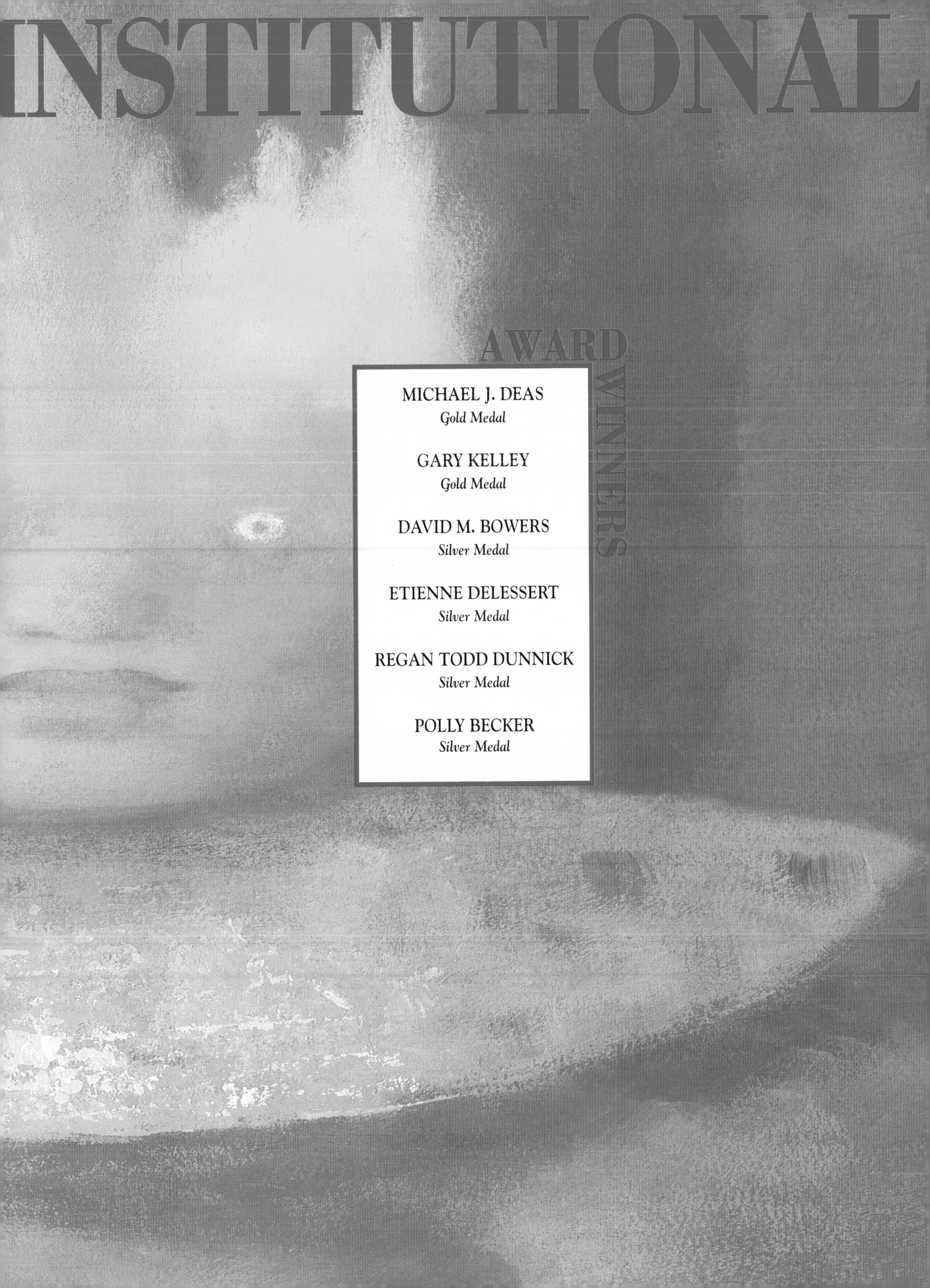

AWARD
WINNERS

MICHAEL J. DEAS
Gold Medal

GARY KELLEY
Gold Medal

DAVID M. BOWERS
Silver Medal

ETIENNE DELESSERT
Silver Medal

REGAN TODD DUNNICK
Silver Medal

POLLY BECKER
Silver Medal

343

Artist: **MICHAEL J. DEAS**

Art Director: Carl Herrman

Client: U.S. Postal Service

Medium: Oil

Size: 10" x 6"

Institutional Gold Medal

MICHAEL J. DEAS

Fresh from his triumphs with the Tennessee Williams and Marilyn Monroe stamps, Michael Deas was assigned by the United States Postal Service to do James Dean as "Rebel Without a Cause." They were looking for the "Fonzie" look, but Michael opted for the dark and brooding side of the actor. He uncovered some rare photographs of Dean, and took over six weeks to create the sketches and finish which were all approved by the Citizens Stamp Advisory Committee and others in Washington, D.C. The diminutive original, an oil on paper, is dictated by the Commission—no more than six times enlarged from its final stamp size.

344

Artist: **GARY KELLEY**

Client: Soho Journal

Medium: Pastel on paper

Size: 28" x 16"

Institutional Gold Medal
GARY KELLEY

"I've been doing this for over twenty years now and I am still amazed that I can have this much fun and somebody will actually pay me for it!"

345

Artist: **DAVID M. BOWERS**

Medium: Oil on masonite

Size: 21 ½" x 15"

Institutional Silver Medal

DAVID BOWERS

Mysterious...Magical...Mystical....rhetorically defines the "Power of the Egg." Maybe it is my imagination, maybe it is the power of positive thinking or maybe it's superstition. Whatever it is, the egg in this picture has power. With complete concentration, I placed the azure, egg-shaped, glass trinket filled with volcanic ash from Mt. Saint Helens on my forehead. I think of an Art Director scanning through the Annual Book and stopping on my page. Subsequently, the Art Director calls me for a job. The egg is my good luck charm, not my inspiration. I am greatly influenced by the Old Masters, particularly Raphael with this piece entitled "Renaissance II."

346

Artist: **ETIENNE DELESSERT**

Art Director: Etienne Delessert

Client: Vallotton Gallery

Medium: Acrylic on tin

Size: 20" x 18"

Institutional Silver Medal
ETIENNE DELESSERT

For Etienne Delessert's most recent exhibition in Switzerland, he created over forty images depicting common phrases. This piece, entitled "Un Ange Passe" ("An Angel Passes"), could be described as that special silence of a crowded room when everyone's sentences end simultaneously, or in the eye of a hurricane or lull in a storm—a temporary hush before the cacophony resumes. Etienne is continuing to use sheets of tin he uncovered in Seymour Chwast's studio. "Paradise," he said, "is only those wonderful precious moments that occur during a long, arduous day, like when an angel passes."

347

Artist: **REGAN TODD DUNNICK**

Art Directors: Chris Hill
          Regan Todd Dunnick

Client: Regan Todd Dunnick

Medium: Pastel

Size: 16" x 22"

Institutional Silver Medal
REGAN TODD DUNNICK

"'Things you would never illustrate' was created as a promotion/self promotion for a Houston-based printer and myself. Chris Hill, my Graphic Design Pal, suggested four small posters that when put together made one large unusual image. This section, `The Moon,' didn't generate much work, but provoked some intriguing calls."

347

348

Artist: **POLLY BECKER**

Art Director: Gigi Fava

Client: Harper's Magazine

Medium: Assemblage

Size: 16" x 10"

Institutional Silver Medal
POLLY BECKER

"For the first several years of my career as an illustrator I was uncomfortable doing people. Working in scratchboard and watercolor, I just tried to the best of my ability to draw things "right"—that is, realistically. When I started experimenting with assemblage, it was extremely liberating. Representing the figure abstractly—in three dimensions, using found objects—I unexpectedly gained access to a new level of emotionality in my work. Assemblage is very much about what is not included. *Restraint*, which comes naturally to me, and is not necessarily an advantage, seems to be required by this medium."

349

Artist: **JAMES R. BENNETT**

Art Director: C. F. Payne

Medium: Oil on board

Size: 9 1/2" x 8"

350

Artist: **MIKE BENNY**

Art Director: Bob Beyn

Agency: Seraphein Beyn

Medium: Acrylic on board

Size: 19" x 16"

351

Artist: **BARRY FITZGERALD**

Medium: Acrylic, colored pencil on
　　　　Bristol board

Size: 12" x 8"

352

Artist: **THOMAS FLUHARTY**

Medium: Acrylic on Bristol

Size: 12 1/2" x 9"

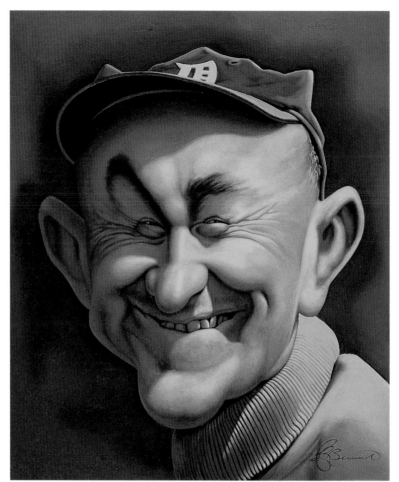

349

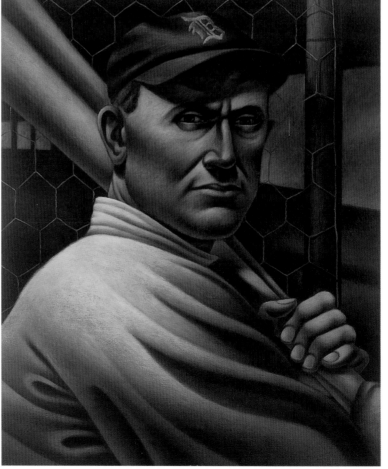

350

351

352

353

Artist: **ROY CARRUTHERS**

Art Director: Alma Phipps

Client: Chief Executive

Medium: Oil on canvas

Size: 16 ¹/₂" x 13 ¹/₂"

354

Artist: **ERIC BOWMAN**

Medium: Acrylic on Crescent board

Size: 9" x 17"

355

Artist: **THOM ANG**

Art Directors: Larry Daley
Elisabeth Vincentelli
Joan Hilty

Client: D.C. Comics

Medium: Mixed

Size: 16" x 11"

356

Artist: **THOM ANG**

Art Director: Gary Gerani

Client: The Topps Co.

Medium: Mixed

Size: 12 ¹/₂" x 9"

353

354

355

356

357

Artist: **BRANT DAY**

Client: Corporate Reports Inc.

Medium: Mixed, collage on Bristol board

Size: 16" x 12"

358

Artist: **PHILIP BLISS**

Medium: Acrylic on canvas

Size: 11" x 15"

359

Artist: **DANIEL ADEL**

Medium: Oil on board

Size: 10 1/2" x 8"

360

Artist: **BRIAN AJHAR**

Art Director: Nick Torello

Client: Scholastic Inc.

Medium: Watercolor

Size: 18" x 13 1/2"

357

358

359

360

361

Artist: **NICK GALIFIANAKIS**

Art Director: Sam Ward

Medium: Watercolor on Bristol board

Size: 12" x 12 ¹/₂"

362

Artist: **RAY-MEL CORNELIUS**

Medium: Acrylic on canvas

Size: 24" x 24"

363

Artist: **LISA FRENCH**

Art Director: Diane Woolverton

Client: U.S. Information Agency

Medium: Acrylic on board

Size: 18 ¹/₂" x 11 ¹/₂"

364

Artist: **SEYMOUR CHWAST**

Art Director: Seymour Chwast

Client: Noblet Serigraphie

Medium: Colored pencil, acrylic on chip board

Size: 17" x 12"

361

362

363

364

365

Artist: **BERNIE FUCHS**

Art Director: Ted Worth

Client: Brooklawn Country Club

Medium: Oil on canvas

Size: 40" x 30"

366

Artist: **BRALDT BRALDS**

Art Director: David Usher

Client: The Greenwich Workshop

Medium: Oil on masonite

Size: 26" x 35 1/2"

367

Artist: **MARK A. BENDER**

Art Director: Cheryl Leto Bender

Client: Broudy Printing Inc.

Medium: Gouache on Strathmore

Size: 8 1/2" x 7"

368

Artist: **JAMES R. BENNETT**

Art Director: C. F. Payne

Medium: Oil on board

Size: 12" x 8 1/2"

365

366

367

368

369

Artist: **ROBERT GIUSTI**

Art Director: Alma Phipps

Client: Chief Executive

Medium: Acrylic on linen

Size: 12" x 12"

370

Artist: **MARY GRANDPRÉ**

Medium: Pastel

Size: 17 1/2" x 17"

371

Artist: **BOB CROFUT**

Art Director: Stan Moberly

Medium: Oil on canvas

Size: 27 1/2" x 35 1/2"

372

Artist: **BILL CIGLIANO**

Art Director: Joe Connolly

Client: Boys' Life

Medium: Oil, gouache on board

Size: 12 1/2" x 22"

369

370

371

372

373

Artist: **MILTON GLASER**

Art Director: Masami Kikuchi

Client: Creation Gallery

Medium: Colored pencil on paper

Size: 14" x 10"

374

Artist: **MICHAEL J. DEAS**

Art Director: Phil Jordan

Client: U.S. Postal Service

Medium: Oil

Size: 5" x 8 ¹/₂"

375

Artist: **CRAIG FRAZIER**

Art Director: Craig Frazier

Client: Oracle

Medium: Iris print

Size: 10" x 8"

376

Artist: **CRAIG FRAZIER**

Art Director: Craig Frazier

Client: Oracle

Medium: Iris print

Size: 14" x 11"

373

374

375

376

377

Artist: **MARK HESS**

Art Director: Dick Sheaff

Client: U.S. Postal Service

Medium: Acrylic on canvas

Size: 5 ¹/₂" x 5"

378

Artist: **MICHAEL KEMPER**

Medium: Ink, gouache, watercolor

Size: 8" x 8"

379

Artist: **REGAN TODD DUNNICK**

Art Directors: Chris Hill
Regan Todd Dunnick

Client: Regan Todd Dunnick

Medium: Pastel

Size: 16" x 22"

380

Artist: **REGAN TODD DUNNICK**

Art Directors: Chris Hill
Regan Todd Dunnick

Client: Regan Todd Dunnick

Medium: Pastel

Size: 18" x 22"

377

378

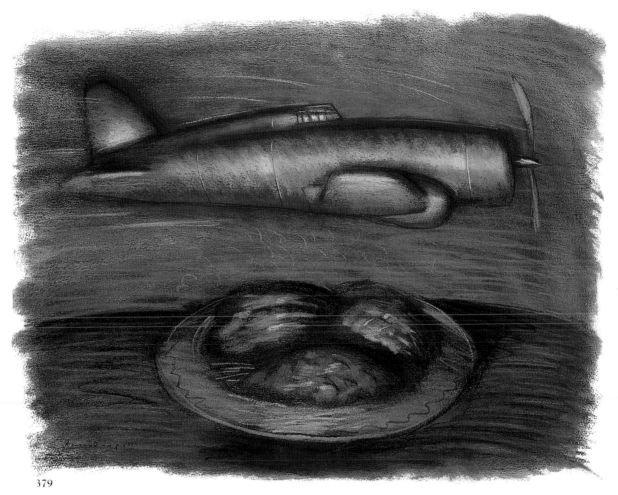

379

380

381

Artist: **MARSHALL ARISMAN**

Art Director: Silas Rhodes

Client: Visual Arts Press

Medium: Oil on canvas

382

Artist: **PETER M. FIORE**

Art Director: Mike Stelzer

Client: Marlin Group

Medium: Oil

Size: 12 ½ " x 28"

383

Artist: **THOM ANG**

Art Director: Gary Gerani

Client: The Topps Co.

Medium: Mixed

Size: 11" x 8"

384

Artist: **JOHN BURGOYNE**

Art Director: John Burgoyne

Client: Katherine Tise

Medium: Ink, watercolor on Strathmore Bristol

Size: 10" x 8"

381

382

383

OSPREY
pandion haliaetus

384

385

Artist: **WILLIAM LOW**

Medium: Oil on paper

Size: 23 1/2" x 21"

386

Artist: **MICHAEL KEMPER**

Medium: Ink, gouache, watercolor

Size: 8" x 8"

387

Artist: **GREG HARGREAVES**

Art Director: Greg Hargreaves

Client: Hellman Assoc.

Medium: Acrylic, color pencil on board

Size: 17 1/2" x 11 1/2"

388

Artist: **LOREN LONG**

Medium: Acrylic on board

Size: 14 1/2 x 10"

385

386

387

388

389

Artist: **BRAD HOLLAND**

Art Director: Janet Longstreth

Client: Neiman Marcus

Medium: Acrylic on masonite

Size: 14" x 12"

390

Artist: **RAFAL OLBINSKI**

Art Director: Rafal Olbinski

Client: Nahan Galleries

Medium: Acrylic on canvas

Size: 30" x 40"

391

Artist: **KATHERINE MAHONEY**

Medium: Mixed

Size: 14 1/2" x 14"

392

Artist: **MICHIKO STEHRENBERGER**

Medium: Croquil pen, Photoshop, Iris Sonerset 300

Size: 25" x 20 1/2"

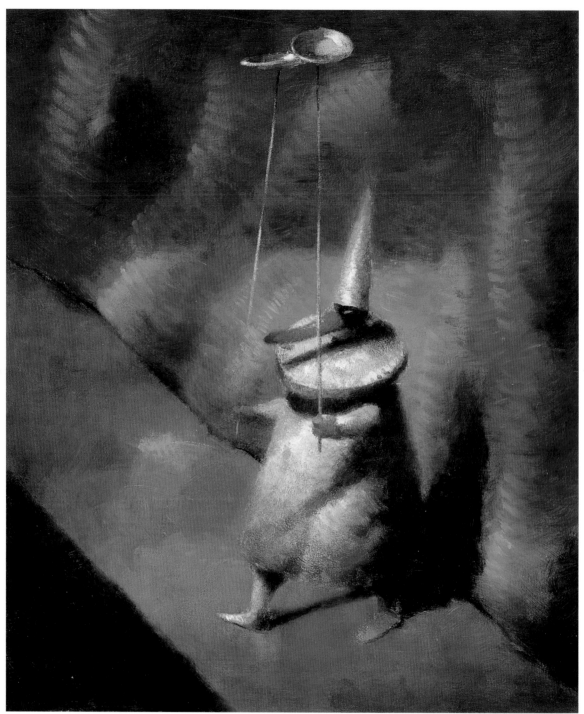

389

390

391

392

393

Artist: **JOANIE SCHWARZ**

Art Director: Don Rosenthal

Client: D. Rosenthal

Medium: Digital work, Painter 3.0

Size: 9" x 9 1/2"

394

Artist: **JOANIE SCHWARZ**

Art Directors: Don Rosenthal

Client: D. Rosenthal

Medium: Digital work, Painter 3.0

Size: 9" x 9"

395

Artist: **BRAD HOLLAND**

Art Director: Robin Ray

Agency: Mad Dog

Client: Seattle Repertory Theatre

Medium: Acrylic on masonite

Size: 12 1/2" x 16"

396

Artist: **DAVID JOHNSON**

Art Director: Richard Solomon

Medium: Pen & ink, watercolor

Size: 10" x 20"

393

394

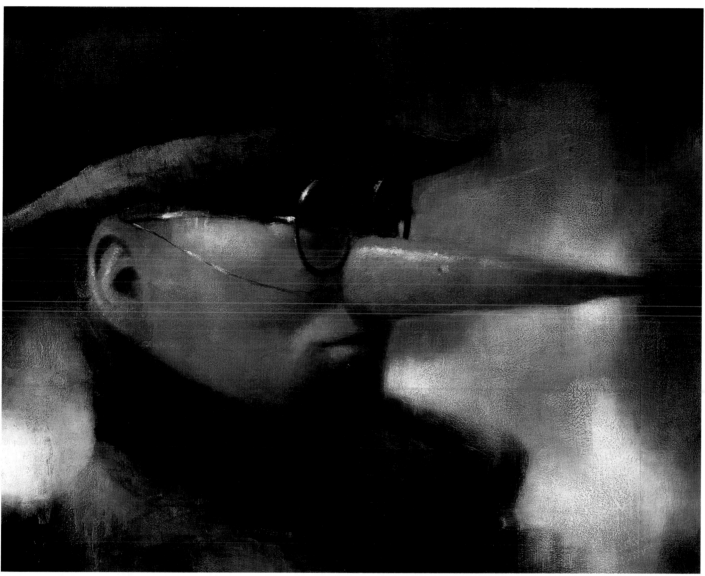

395

396

397

Artist: **JAMES GURNEY**

Art Director: David Usher

Client: The Greenwich Workshop

Medium: Oil on canvas

Size: 39 1/2" x 23 1/2"

398

Artist: **DICK COLE**

Art Director: Jon Wells

Client: San Francisco Society of Illustrators

Medium: Watercolor

Size: 13 1/2" x 10 1/2"

399

Artist: **RAY-MEL CORNELIUS**

Medium: Acrylic on canvas

Size: 34" x 24"

400

Artist: **MARK ENGLISH**

Art Director: Tim Trabon

Client: Trabon Paris Printing

Medium: Pastel on paper

Size: 18 1/2" x 23 1/2"

397

398

399

400

401

Artist: **ROBERT RAYEVSKY**

Art Director: Mark Von Ulrich

Client: Black Book Marketing Group, Inc.

Medium: Hand-colored hard ground etching

Size: 11 1/2" x 8 1/2"

402

Artist: **LARRY MOORE**

Art Director: Jeff Morris

Client: Resort Design/Walt Disney World

Medium: Pastel on sanded paper

Size: 16" x 18"

403

Artist: **ANN GLOVER**

Client: Grace Godlin

Medium: Oil on masonite

Size: 13 1/2" x 15"

404

Artist: **ANN GLOVER**

Medium: Oil on masonite

Size: 9" x 12"

401

402

403

404

405

Artist: **ETIENNE DELESSERT**

Art Director: Etienne Delessert

Client: Vallotton Gallery

Medium: Acrylic on tin

Size: 20" x 18"

406

Artist: **ETIENNE DELESSERT**

Art Director: Etienne Delessert

Client: Vallotton Gallery

Medium: Acrylic on tin

Size: 20" x 18"

407

Artist: **GARY KELLEY**

Art Director: Craig Bernhard

Client: Republic National Bank of New York

Medium: Pastel on paper

Size: 14 1/2" x 42"

408

Artist: **ALBERT LORENZ**

Art Director: Albert Lorenz

Client: MTB Bank /York Graphic
Communication

Medium: Mixed on Bristol

Size: 29" x 39"

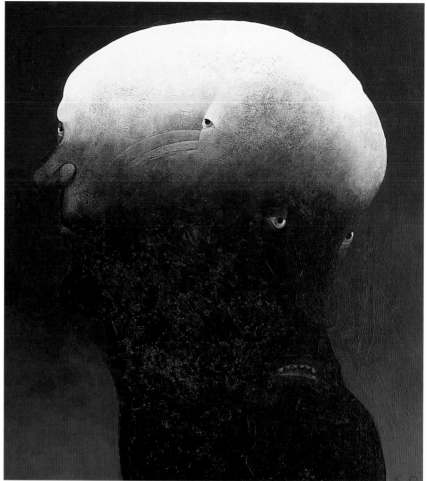

405

406

407

408

409

Artist: **VICTOR GADINO**

Medium: Oil on canvas

Size: 30" x 24"

410

Artist: **TRACY COX**

Medium: Conte crayon, collage on paper

Size: 10" x 8"

411

Artist: **MARY GRANDPRÉ**

Medium: Gouache, pastel on paper

Size: 21 1/2" x 16"

412

Artist: **ANN GLOVER**

Art Directors: Morton Kaish
Lynn Pearl

Client: Winsor & Newton

Medium: Oil on masonite

Size: 9" x 12"

409

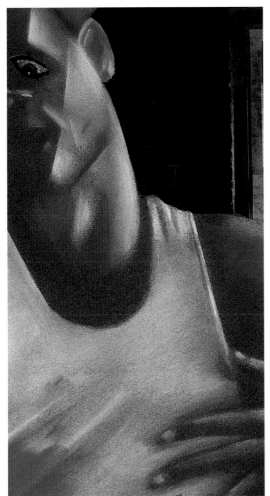

410

411

412

413

Artist: **PHILIP STRAUB**

Medium: Oil on board

Size: 15" x 13"

414

Artist: **CYNTHIA von BUHLER**

Art Director: Josephine Di Donato

Client: Sony Records

Medium: Mixed with live dove on canvas
and wood

Size: 28" x 28"

415

Artist: **PAUL KRATTER**

Art Director: Bette Trono

Client: Portal Publications Inc.

Medium: Acrylic on board

Size: 21" x 32"

416

Artist: **FRANCIS LIVINGSTON**

Art Director: William Dunn

Client: Reynold Fine Art

Medium: Oil on board

Size: 14" x 18"

413

414

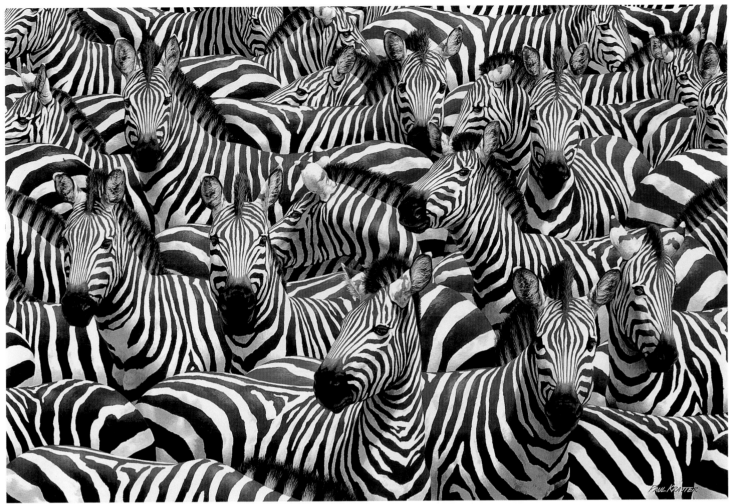

415

416

417

Artist: **HIRO KIMURA**

Art Director: Ira Goldstein

Client: Jerry's Artarama, Inc.

Medium: Acrylic on board

Size: 16" x 13"

418

Artist: **GARY LOCKE**

Medium: Watercolor

Size: 12 ¹/₂" x 17 ¹/₂"

419

Artist: **JOHN CRAIG**

Art Director: Jon Flaming

Client: Wilson Engraving Co., Inc.

Medium: Collage

Size: 13" x 10"

420

Artist: **DAVE CUTLER**

Art Director: Mark Tarry

Agency: Harmon Smith Advertising

Client: Hill Pet Co.

Medium: Acrylic on paper

Size: 8" x 6"

417

418

419

420

421

Artist: **JOHN JUDE PALENCAR**

Art Directors: George Cornell
Jerry Todd

Client: Penguin USA

Medium: Acrylic on panel

Size: 27 ¹/₂" x 24 ¹/₂"

422

Artist: **PHILIP STRAUB**

Medium: Oil on board

Size: 15" x 12"

423

Artist: **DAVE La FLEUR**

Art Director: Lydia Anderson

Client: GTE

Medium: Oil on linen

Size: 16 ¹/₂" x 22"

424

Artist: **GARY HEAD**

Client: Hallmark Cards

Medium: Acrylic on watercolor board

Size: 9" x 14"

421

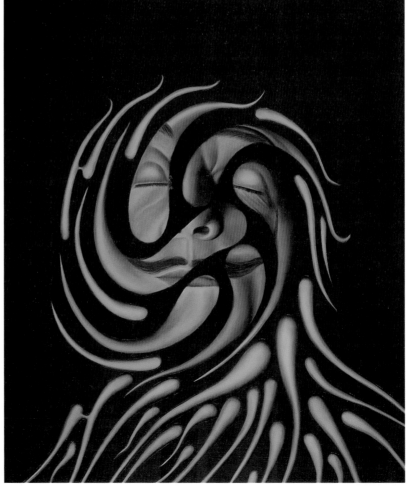

422

423

424

425

Artist: **FRED SMITH**

Medium: Oil, acrylic on board

Size: 17 1/2" x 13"

426

Artist: **JULIE MAMMANO**

Art Director: Linda Fong

Client: Caravan International, Inc.

Medium: Watercolor on Arches

Size: 24" x 38"

427

Artist: **WILSON McLEAN**

Art Director: Chris Hill

Client: Hines Interests Limited
       Partnership

Medium: Oil on canvas

Size: 39 1/2" x 22 1/2"

428

Artist: **ROBERT McGINNIS**

Client: Hunterdon Art Center

Medium: Oil on gessoed panel

Size: 24" x 15"

425

426

427

428

429

Artist: **DAVID WILCOX**

Art Director: Chris Passehl

Client: Keiler & Co.

Medium: Casein, acrylic on board

Size: 15" x 14"

430

Artist: **DAVID WILCOX**

Art Director: Chris Passehl

Client: Keiler & Co.

Medium: Casein, acrylic on board

Size: 15" x 14"

431

Artist: **BILL MAYER**

Art Director: Dick Henderson

Agency: Cole Henderson Drake

Client: Georgia-Pacific Papers

Medium: Airbrush, gouache,
　　　dyes on Strathmore

Size: 11" x 14 1/2"

432

Artist: **DAVE McKEAN**

Art Director: Dave McKean

Client: Allen Spiegel Fine Arts

Medium: Mixed, Mac computer

Size: 10" x 16"

429

430

431

432

433

Artist: **JACK N. UNRUH**

Art Director: Jack Summerford

Client: Society of Illustrators

Medium: Ink, watercolor on board

Size: 11" x 11"

434

Artist: **JANE SANDERS**

Art Director: Laurie Hinzman

Client: Nickelodeon

Medium: Iris printout, Illustrator 5.5 Macintosh

Size: 10 1/2" x 14"

435

Artist: **JOHN P. MAGGARD III**

Art Directors: Kris Schwandner
Cliff Schwandner

Client: Cincinnati Heart Assn.

Medium: Acrylic, ink, oil on

Strathmore

Size: 27" x 12"

436

Artist: **C. MICHAEL DUDASH**

Medium: Oil on linen

Size: 13 1/2" x 20"

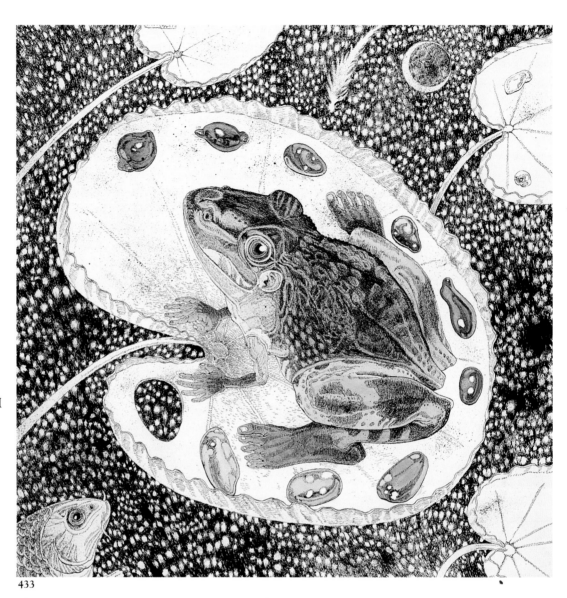

433

434

435

436

437

Artist: **GENNADY SPIRIN**

Art Director: Bea Jackson

Client: Wild Honey

Medium: Watercolor

Size: 11 3/8" x 8 7/8"

438

Artist: **LORA YAKIMOW**

Art Director: James Etling

Agency: LoraJean Co.

Client: Eye of the Lizard Gallery

Medium: Oil on canvas

Size: 30" x 54"

439

Artist: **JACK E. DAVIS**

Art Director: Richard Solomon

Medium: Colored pencil on board

Size: 11" x 8"

440

Artist: **MARY GRANDPRÉ**

Medium: Pastel on paper

Size: 22 1/2" x 17"

437

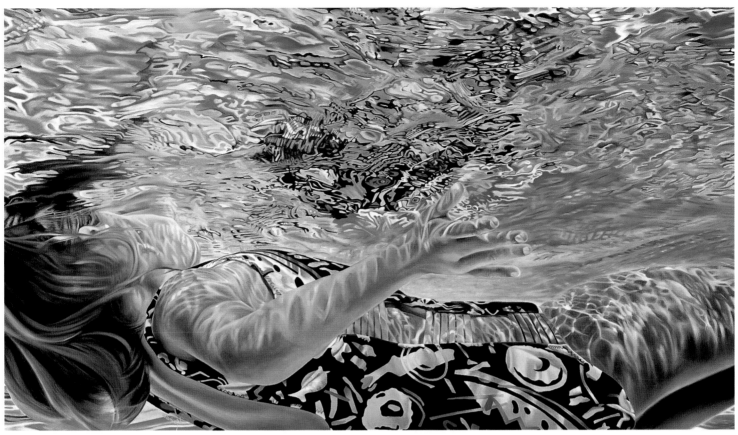

438

439

440

441

Artist: **ROBERT RODRIGUEZ**

Art Director: Jeff Labbé

Client: Society of Illustrators of
Los Angeles

Medium: Oil on wood panel

Size: 20" x 13 ½"

442

Artist: **DAN YACCARINO**

Medium: Watercolor on paper

Size: 8" x 11"

443

Artist: **ROBERT RAYEVSKY**

Art Director: Robert Rayevsky

Medium: Mixed

Size: 11 ½" x 9"

444

Artist: **NATHAN T. OTA**

Medium: Acrylic on board

Size: 11" x 8 ½"

441

442

443

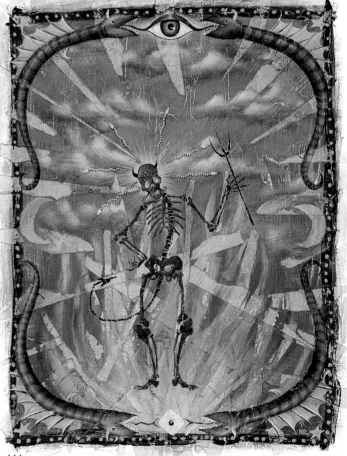

444

445

Artist: **WILL WILSON**

Medium: Oil on canvas

446

Artist: **MICHAEL D. RYUS**

Art Directors: Christopher Hadden
Michael D. Ryus

Client: Portland Landmarks Society

Medium: Oil and varnish on
composite neg. photograph

447

Artist: **JOHN RUSH**

Art Director: John Rush

Client: Eleanor Ettinger Gallery

Medium: Oil on canvas

Size: 24" x 16"

448

Artist: **TRICIA TUSA**

Medium: Acrylic on masonite

Size: 14" x 8"

445

446

447

448

449

Artist: **ROB WOOD**

Client: Wildlife Natural Care Center

Medium: Acrylic on board

Size: 20" x 15"

450

Artist: **ROBERT LYNCH**

Art Director: Kelly Ludwig

Client: Ludwig Design, Inc.

Medium: Oil pastel on masonite

Size: 48" x 32"

451

Artist: **TED WRIGHT**

Art Director: Kelley Hyde

Client: Yupper Westside

Medium: Poster inks

Size: 23 ¹/₂" x 12 ¹/₂"

452

Artist: **CRAIG FRAZIER**

Art Director: Craig Frazier

Client: The Energy Foundation

Medium: Iris print

Size: 11" x 14"

449

450

451

452

453

Artist: **WILL WILSON**

Medium: Oil on canvas

Size: 18" x 14"

454

Artist: **TOM HENNESSY**

Art Director: Jim Moon

Client: Real Restaurants

Medium: Gouache on clayboard

Size: 4" x 6"

455

Artist: **C.F. PAYNE**

Art Director: Serge Michaels

Client: Society of Illustrators of
Los Angeles

Medium: Mixed

Size: 15" x 10"

456

Artist: **CURTIS PARKER**

Art Director: Chris Ray

Client: Everest Publishing Co.

Medium: Acrylic on linen

Size: 23 1/2" x 17 1/2"

453

454

455

456

457

Artist: **PATRICK D. MILBOURN**

Medium: Oil on wood panel

Size: 12" x 10"

458

Artist: **JOHN THOMPSON**

Medium: Acrylic on chipboard

Size: 9 1/2" x 7"

459

Artist: **THOMAS KLAR**

Medium: Acrylic on board

Size: 30" x 20"

460

Artist: **BART FORBES**

Client: Bruce McGaw Graphics

Medium: Oil on canvas

Size: 31" x 21 1/2"

457

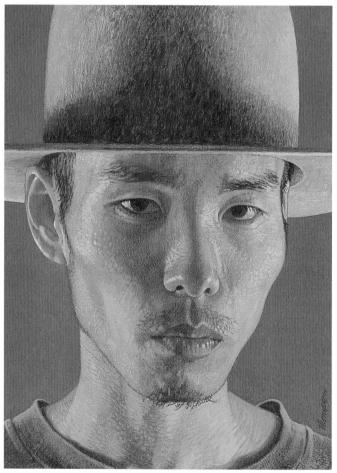

458

459

460

461

Artist: **GARY KELLEY**

Art Director: Richard Solomon

Medium: Pastel on paper

Size: 17 1/2" x 14 1/2"

462

Artist: **LARRY MOORE**

Art Director: Meredith Rushing

Client: Central Florida Press

Medium: Pastel

Size: 6" x 20"

463

Artist: **THOMAS THRUN**

Medium: Oil on paper

Size: 14" x 10 1/2"

464

Artist: **STANLEY (OLSEN) FELLOWS**

Medium: Watercolor

Size: 11" x 8 1/2"

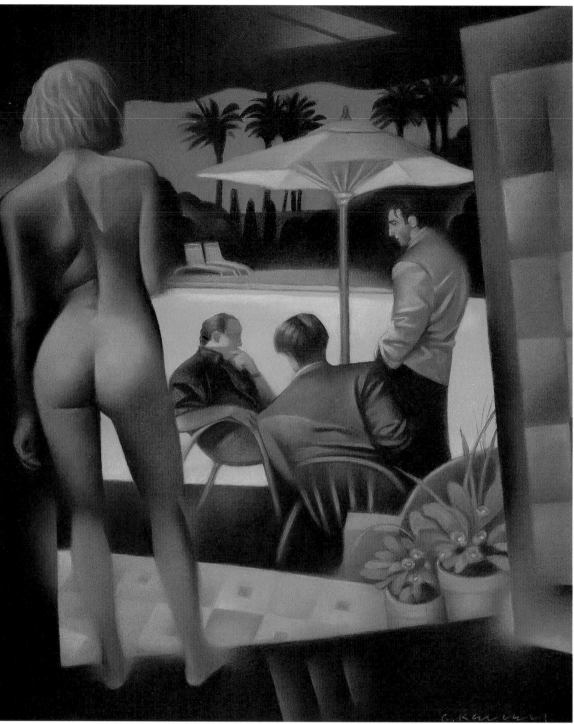

461

462

463

464

465

Artist: **JOSÉ ORTEGA**

Medium: Mixed on paper

Size: 12" x 9 1/2"

466

Artist: **CLIFFORD FAUST**

Medium: Collage

Size: 20 1/2" x 19"

467

Artist: **WILSON McLEAN**

Art Director: Kerig Pope

Client: Playboy

Medium: Oil on canvas

Size: 20" x 23 1/2"

468

Artist: **FRED OTNES**

Art Director: John deCesare

Medium: Mixed, collage on linen canvas

Size: 12" x 14"

465

466

467

468

469

Artist: **MICHAEL J. DEAS**

Art Directors: Ray D'Amelio
Lauren Sachs

Agency: Bates, U.S.A.

Client: U.S. Armed Forces

Medium: Oil on panel

Size: 17" x 19"

470

Artist: **KELLY STRIBLING SUTHERLAND**

Art Director: Eddie Nunns

Client: Neiman Marcus

Medium: Acrylic, oil on board

Size: 22" x 18"

471

Artist: **DAN YACCARINO**

Client: Paper Moon

Medium: Oil on canvas

Size: 19" x 15"

472

Artist: **PHILIPPE LARDY**

Medium: Watercolor, ink

Size: 11" x 13"

469

470

471

472

473

Artist: **JAMES R. BENNETT**

Medium: Oil on board

Size: 23 1/2" x 16 1/2"

474

Artist: **BILL MAYER**

Art Director: Dick Henderson

Agency: Cole Henderson Drake

Client: Georgia-Pacific Papers

Medium: Pastel on paper

Size: 11 1/2" x 15"

475

Artist: **DOUGLAS SMITH**

Medium: Scratchboard, watercolor

Size: 13 1/2" x 10"

476

Artists: **STEVE JOHNSON**
LOU FANCHER

Art Director: Doug Joseph

Client: SCE Corp.

Medium: Acrylic on gessoed paper

Size: 14" x 11"

473

474

475

476

477

Artist: **CATHLEEN TOELKE**

Art Director: Ron Toelke

Client: Creative Connections

Medium: Gouache on board

Size: 11 ¹/₂" x 9"

478

Artist: **REGAN TODD DUNNICK**

Art Director: Karen Schlossberg

Client: The Bureau of National Affairs, Inc.

Medium: Pastel

Size: 8" x 6"

479

Artists: **STEVE JOHNSON LOU FANCHER**

Medium: Acrylic on canvas

Size: 30" x 22"

480

Artist: **BOB DACEY**

Art Director: Joe Glisson

Client: Dellas Graphics

Medium: Watercolor on Strathmore board

Size: 22" x 17"

477

478

479

480

481

Artist: **WILSON McLEAN**

Art Directors: Kerig Pope

Client: Playboy

Medium: Oil on canvas

Size: 19 ¹/₂" x 19 ¹/₂"

481-A

Artist: **DOUGLAS SMITH**

Medium: Scratchboard

Size: 12" x 10"

482

Artist: **PHILIPPE LARDY**

Art Director: John Klotnia

Client: Rohr-Poulenc

Medium: Watercolor, gouache on paper

Size: 12" x 9"

483

Artist: **ELVIS SWIFT**

Art Directors: Ray Fesenmeier

Client: Karg Fesenmeier

Medium: Ink on paper

Size: 8 ¹/₂" x 11"

484

Artist: **LINDA HELTON**

Art Director: Susie Stockard

Client: Federal Reserve Bank of Dallas

Medium: Acrylic, ink

Size: 11" x 9 ¹/₂"

481

481-A

482

483

484

INTERNATIONAL JURY

BRIAN CRONIN
Illustrator

MIRKO ILIC
Illustrator

DOUG JOHNSON
Illustrator

HIRO KIMURA
Illustrator

SOREN NORING
Art Director
Reader's Digest

INTERNATIONAL

485

Artist: **FERNANDO BUIGUES**

Art Directors: Marcelo Vergara
Fabio Mazia

Client: Pizza Piola

Medium: Acrylic

Size: 35cm x 27cm

486

Artist: **MICHAEL BRAMMAN**

Art Director: Claire Ward

Client: Transworld Publishers Ltd.

Medium: Acrylic

Size: 48cm x 62.5cm

487

Artist: **BJORN MIKE BOGE**

Art Director: Eirik Moe

Client: Phillips

Medium: Mixed

Size: 17cm x 40cm

488

Artist: **WARABE ASKA**

Art Director: Warabe Aska

Client: Delacorte Press Bantam
Doubleday

Medium: Oil on canvas

Size: 28cm x 56cm

485

486

487

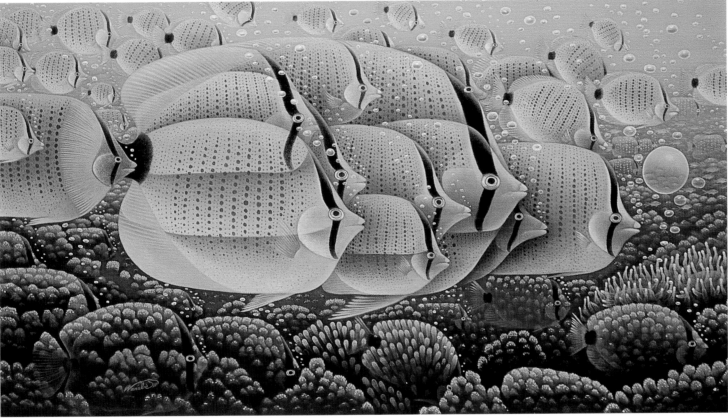

488

489

Artist: **ULISES CULEBRO**

Art Director: Magu

Client: El Papa del Ahuizote

Medium: Ink on paper

Size: 14cm x 8cm

490

Artist: **JOVAN DJORDJEVIC**

Art Director: Lisa Clark

Client: The Independent on Sunday

Medium: Montage, ink, photo dye

Size: 17cm x 22cm

491

Artist: **HARVEY CHAN**

Client: Groundwood Books

Medium: Oil on canvas

Size: 60cm x 45cm

492

Artist: **HARVEY CHAN**

Client: Groundwood Books

Medium: Oil on canvas

Size: 60cm x 45cm

493

Artist: **JOVAN DJORDJEVIC**

Art Director: Lisa Clark

Client: The Independent on Sunday

Medium: Montage, ink, photo dye

Size: 17cm x 26cm

489

490

491

492

493

494

Artist: **JOVAN DJORDJEVIC**

Art Director: Roger Browning

Client: Guardian Newspaper - Online

Medium: Montage, ink, photo dye

Size: 22cm x 27cm

495

Artist: **TADAO FURUTA**

Art Director: Fumio Ichihara

Client: Nissan Graphic Arts Co. Ltd.

Size: 58cm x 50cm

496

Artist: **ANDREJ DUGIN**

Art Director: B.A. Diodorov

Client: Detskaja Literatura

Medium: Watercolor

Size: 26.5cm x 41.5cm

497

Artist: **ANDREJ DUGIN**

Art Director: B.A. Diodorov

Client: Detskaja Literatura

Medium: Watercolor

Size: 26.5cm x 41.5cm

494

495

496

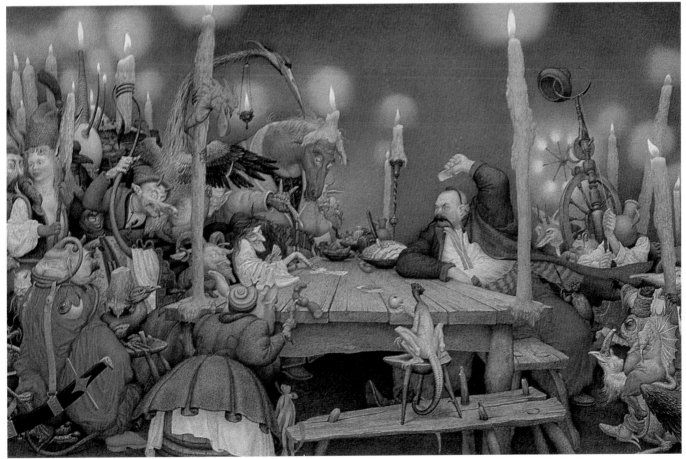

497

498

Artist: **JAMES MARSH**

Art Director: Terry Hedges

Client: Personal Computer Magazine

Medium: Acrylic

Size: 35cm x 45cm

499

Artist: **HIDEKI MABUCHI**

Art Director: Masakazu Tanabe

Client: Central

Medium: Acrylic on illustration board

Size: 57cm x 39cm

500

Artist: **NOBUO KUSUNOKI**

Art Director: Toru Osabe

Client: Maxell

Size: 19cm x 25cm

501

Artist: **OTMAR GRISSEMANN**

Art Director: Otmar Grissemann

Medium: Airbrush, colored pencil

Size: 59cm x 42cm

502

Artist: **NOBUO KUSUNOKI**

Art Director: Yoshinori Kawabata

Client: Nippon Glaxo

498

499

500

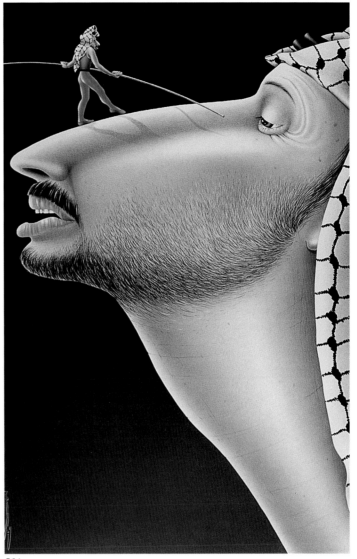

501

502

503

Artist: **NORIKO HATANO**

Art Director: Tomoyuki Adachi

Client: Bunen-sha

Size: 30cm x 20cm

504

Artist: **TOYOTSUGU ITOH**

Art Director: Toyotsugu Itoh

Client: Mainichi Newspapers

Size: 103cm x 73cm

505

Artist: **PIERRE-PAUL PARISEAU**

Art Director: Carmen Dunjko

Client: Saturday Night Magazine

Medium: Photo collage

Size: 25cm x 34cm

506

Artist: **TOYOTSUGU ITOH**

Art Director: Toyotsugu Itoh

Client: Gate Exhibition
Executive Committee

Size: 103cm x 73cm

507

Artist: **NOBUO KUSUNOKI**

Art Director: Ohmizota Design Office

Client: Toto

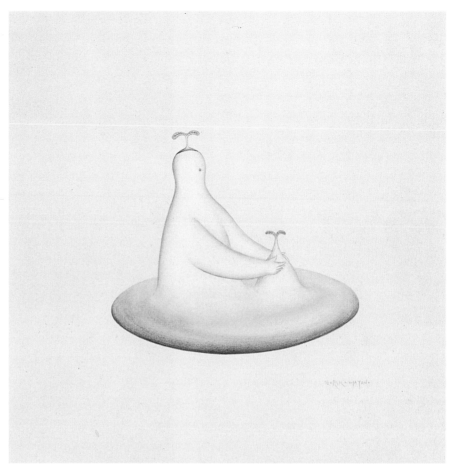

503

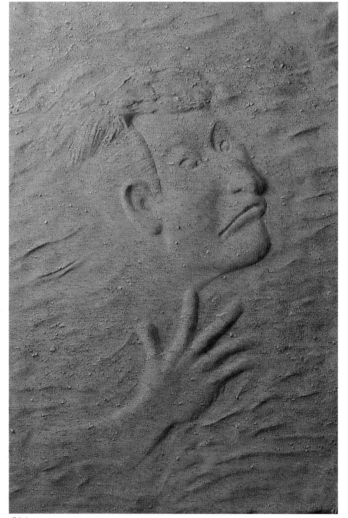

504

505

506

507

508

Artist: **HITOSHI MIURA**

Art Director: Motomitsu Takagi

Size: 103cm x 73cm

509

Artist: **HITOSHI MIURA**

Art Director: Hitoshi Miura

Client: Miura Creations

Size: 15cm x 10.5cm

510

Artist: **HITOSHI MIURA**

Art Director: Hitoshi Miura

Client: Miura Creations

Size: 15cm x 10.5cm

511

Artist: **VICTORIA MARTOS**

Art Director: Carmelo Caderot

Client: El Mundo

Medium: Acrylic

Size: 40cm x 30cm

512

Artist: **DUSAN PETRICIC**

Art Director: Ian Somerville

Client: Toronto Star

Size: 20cm x 35cm

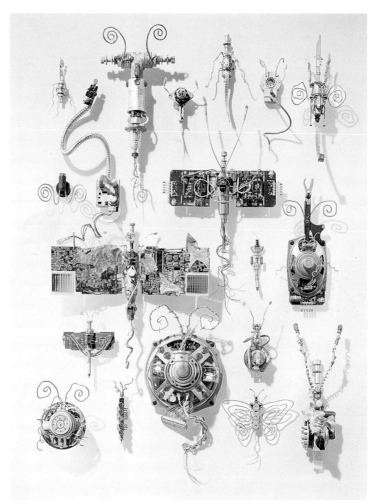

508

509

CRAFTRATION:HITOSHI MIURA(MIURA CREATION) PHOTO:KAZUAKI FUTAZUKA(AGNI STUDIO)

510

511

512

513

Artist: **RICK SEALOCK**

Art Director: Rick Sealock

Client: Maverick Art Tribe

Medium: Acryllic

Size: 64cm x 60cm

514

Artist: **RICK SEALOCK**

Art Director: Gavin Orpren

Client: BC Business Magazine

Medium: Acryllic

Size: 32cm x 32cm

515

Artist: **JOSE PEREZ MONTERO**

Client: Scandinavia Publishing House

Size: 37cm x 49cm

516

Artist: **DUSAN PETRICIC**

Art Director: Dusan Petricic

Client: Kids Can Press

Size: 31cm x 65cm

513

514

515

516

517
Artist: **JURGEN MICK**

Medium: Colored pencil

Size: 40cm x 36cm

518
Artist: **ALBERT ROCAROLS**

Art Director: Xavier Corretje

Client: Guarro Casas S.A.

Medium: Acrylic

Size: 70cm x 100cm

519
Artist: **RICK SEALOCK**

Art Director: Rick Sealock

Client: Maverick Art Tribe

Medium: Acrylic

Size: 76cm x 51cm

520
Artist: **MARC MCBRIDE**

Art Director: Paul Collins

Client: Sumeria Publishing

Medium: Acrylic

Size: 74cm x 48cm

521
Artist: **KEIKO SHINDO**

Art Director: Norihisa Tojinbara

Client: Genkosha

Size: 36cm x 51cm

517

518

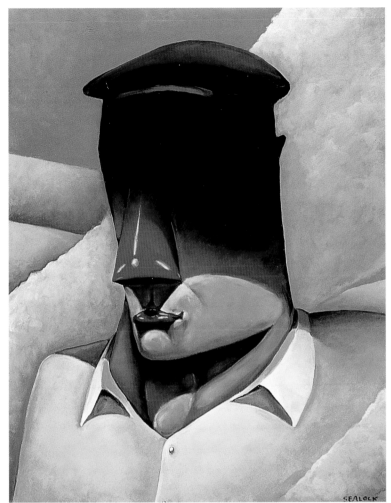

519

520

521

522

Artist: ASTRIO
SKAAREN-FVSTRO

Size: 40cm x 50cm

523

Artist: ASTRIO
SKAAREN-FVSTRO

Size: 25cm x 25cm

524

Artist: FLETCHER SIBTHORP

Art Director: Mark Skelton

Client: Iberia Airways

Medium: Mixed on canvas

Size: 79cm x 59cm

525

Artist: FLETCHER SIBTHORP

Art Director: Alison Pincott

Client: ES Magazine

Medium: Mixed on canvas

Size: 94cm x 74cm

522

523

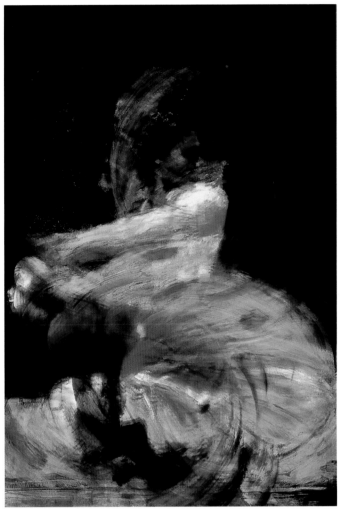

524

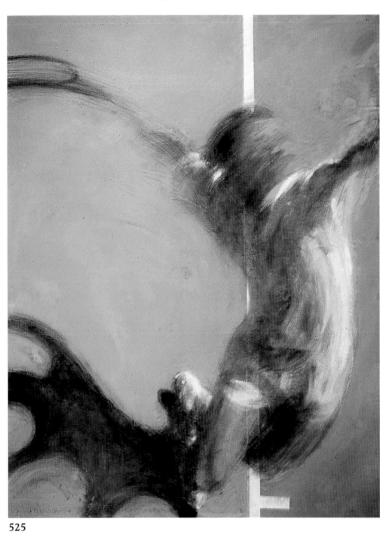

525

526

Artist: **ASTRIO SKAAREN FVSTRO**

Size: 25cm x 25cm

527

Artist: **BEN TOMITA**

Art Director: Ben Tomita

Client: Orgao Inc.

Medium: Paper, concrete

Size: 40cm x 45cm

528

Artist: **YASUTAKA TAGA**

Art Director: Yasutaka Taga

Client: Dosv User Magazine

Medium: Clay, acrylic, computer

Size: 29cm x 21cm

529

Artist: **YASUTAKA TAGA**

Art Director: Yasutaka Taga

Client: Dosv User Magazine

Medium: Clay, acrylic, computer, stone

Size: 29cm x 21cm

526

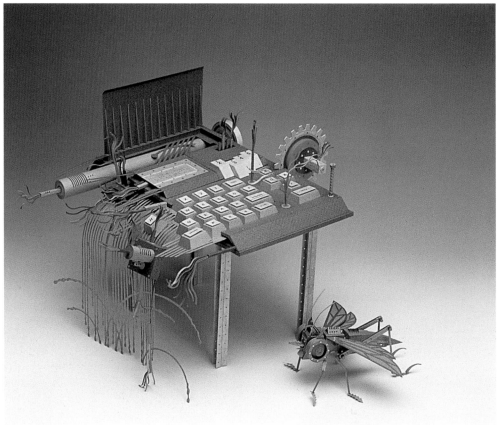

527

528

529

530

Artist: **FUMIO WATANABE**

Art Director: Noriyuki IIjima

Client: Yomiuri Newspaper Publisher

Size: 45cm x 50cm

531

Artist: **FUMIO WATANABE**

Art Director: Noriyuki IIjima

Client: Yomiuri Newspaper Publisher

Size: 45cm x 50cm

532

Artist: **BEN TOMITA**

Art Director: Yoshiko Watanabe

Client: Recruit Co. Ltd.

Medium: Paper, concrete

Size: 50cm x 40cm

533

Artist: **YASUTAKA TAGA**

Art Director: Yasutaka Taga

Client: Dosv User Magazine

Medium: Clay, acrylic, computer

Size: 27cm x 21cm

530

531

532

533

534

Artist: **BRAD YEO**

Art Director: Louis Krynski

Client: DowElanco

Medium: Acrylic

Size: 56cm x 38cm

535

Artist: **HIROMITSU YOKOTA**

Medium: Gouache on paper

Size: 30cm x 21cm

536

Artist: **BRAD YEO**

Art Director: Brad Yeo

Medium: Acrylic

Size: 46cm x 163cm

537

Artist: **HIROSHI WATANABE**

Art Director: Toshikazu Ohta

Client: CBS Sony

Size: 50cm x 30cm

538

Artist: **KIYOKA YAMAZUKI**

Art Director: Motosi Kuroda

Client: Nagoya City

Size: 103cm x 72.5cm

534

535

536

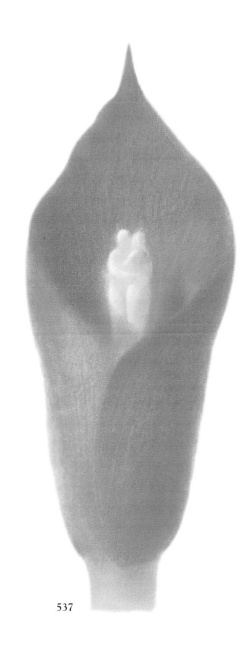

537

538

ARTIST INDEX

ARTIST INDEX

Mayer, Bill, 233, 286, 287, 315,
431, 474
240 Forkner Dr.
Decatur, GA 30030
(404) 378-0686

McCauley, Adam, 199, 318
2400 Eighth Ave.
Oakland, CA 94606
(510) 832-0860

McGinnis, Robert, 428
13 Arcadia Rd.
Old Greenwich, CT 06870
(203) 637-5055

McKean, Dave, 176, 432
c/o Allen Spiegel
221 Lobos Ave.
Pacific Grove, CA 93950
(408) 372-4672
Rep: Allen Spiegel (408) 372-4672

McLean, Wilson, 42, 427, 467, 481
27 Montauk Hwy., Art Village
Southampton, NY 11968
(516) 283-4276

McMullan, James, 53, 222
207 E. 32nd St.
New York, NY 10016
(212) 689-5527

Meehan, Maureen, 183
(212) 343-1260

Meek, James Gordon, 325
P.O. Box 27762
Washington, DC 20038
(703) 734-3385

Merkin, Richard, 87
500 West End Ave. #12D
New York, NY 10024
(212) 724-9285

Milbourn, Patrick D., 457
327 W. 22nd St.
New York, NY 10011
(212) 989-4594

Minor, Wendell, 202, 203
15 Old North Rd.
Washington, CT 06793
(860) 868-9101

Moore, Larry, 402, 462
1635 Delaney Ave.
Orlando, FL 32806
(407) 648-0832
Rep: (212) 677-9100

Murdocca, Salvatore, 197
95 Horatio St.
New York, NY 10014
(212) 807-0709

Muth, Jon J., 211
c/o Allen Spiegel
221 Lobos Ave.
Pacific Grove, CA 93950
(408) 372-4672
Rep: Allen Spiegel (408) 372-4672

Nakamura, Joel, 269
221 W. Maple
Monrovia, CA 91016
(818) 301-0177

Nass, Rhonda, 258, 259
4130 Barlow Rd.
Cross Plains, WI 53528
(608) 798-3500
Rep: Kastaris (314) 773-2600

Nelson, Will, 323
1053 Saranal Dr.
Boise, IO 83709
(208) 375-2901

Nesbitt, James, 306
Wall-toWall Studios, Inc.
The Crane Bldg., 40 24th St.
Pittsburgh, PA 15222
(412) 232-0880

Newbold, Greg, 205
1231 E. 6600 S.
Salt Lake City, UT 84121
(801) 268-2209

Newman, Bob, 108
11 Eagle Rock Hill
Centerport, NY 11721
(516) 754-2475

Nielsen, Cliff, 208
9044 E. Ardendale Ave.
San Gabriel, CA 91775
(818) 285-9966

Niklewicz, Adam, 263
44 Great Quarter Rd.
Sandy Hook, CT 06482
(203) 270-8424

Ning, Amy, 36
1442 Freeman Ave.
Long Beach, CA 90804
(310) 498-2273

Northeast, Christian, 285
10 Beaconsfield Ave. #3
Toronto, Ontario Canada M6J 3H9
(416) 538-0400

O'Brien, Tim, 266
480 13th St.
Brooklyn, NY 11215
(718) 832-1287

Olbinski, Rafal, 132, 282, 283,
322, 390
142 E. 35th St.
New York, NY 10016
(212) 532-4328

O'Neal, Lamont, 334
318 W. 14th St. #2
New York, NY 10014
(212) 924-1210

Ortega, José, 465
131 Ave. B #1C
New York, NY 10009
(212) 228-2606

Ota, Nathan T., 444
963 5th Ave.
Los Angeles, CA 90019
(213) 934-1741

Otnes, Fred, 141, 153, 468
26 Chalburn Rd.
West Redding, CT 06896
(203) 938-2829

Palencar, John Jude, 145, 152,
168, 421
249 Elm St.
Oberlin, OH 44074
(216) 774-7312

Palmer, Randy, 22
37 S. Ludlow St.
Dayton, OH 45402
(513) 225-2386

Pappalardo, Dean, 299
Modino Design
225 Lafayette St.
New York, NY 10012
(212) 431-4354

Paraskevas, Michael, 49, 50, 90
157 Tuckahoe Ln.
Southampton, NY 11068
(516) 287-1665

Parker, Curtis, 456
1946 E. Palomino Dr.
Tempe, AZ 85284
(602) 820-6015

Parker, Robert Andrew, 88, 106,
107
22 River Rd.
West Cornwall, CT 06796
(203) 672-0152

Patrick, John, 101
555 Tusculum Ave.
Cincinnati, OH 45226
(513) 871-6017
Rep. (513) 433-8383

Payne, C.F., 69, 77, 93, 455
758 Springfield Pike
Cincinnati, OH 45215
(513) 821-8009

Pendleton, Roy, 210
28 Pimlico Dr.
Commack, NY 11725
(516) 543-0003

Pinkney, Jerry, 112, 126, 166, 167
41 Furnace Dock Rd.
Croton-on-Hudson
NY 10520
(914) 271-5238

Podevin, Jean François, 215
5812 Newlin Ave.
Whittier, CA 90601
(310) 945-9613

Polson, Steven, 214
225 E. 79th St.
New York, NY 10021
(212) 734-3917

Porfirio, Guy, 337
4101 E. Holmes
Tucson, AZ 85711
(520) 881-7708

Pugliese, Christopher, 181
611 Adams St.
Hoboken, NJ 07030
(201) 222-8128

Ransome, James, 160, 161, 227
71 Hooker Ave.
Poughkeepsie, NY 12601
(914) 473-8281

Rayevsky, Robert, 401, 443
1120 Swedesford Rd.
North Wales, PA 19454
(215) 661-9566
Rep: (415) 285-8267

Riedy, Mark, 320
Scott Hull Assoc.
68 E. Franklin St.
Centerville, OH 45459
(513) 433-7174
Rep: (513) 433-8383

Rodriguez, Robert, 441
2408 Paloma St.
Pasadena, CA 91104
(818) 794-2628
Rep: Renard Represents
(212) 490-2450

Rush, John, 267, 447
123 Kedzie St.
Evanston, IL 60202
(847) 869-2078

Ryus, Michael D., 446
4 Waverly Rd.
Cape Elizabeth, ME 04107
(207) 767-2228

Sadowski, Wiktor, 4, 307
c/o Marlena Torzecka
211 E. 89th St. #A1
New York, NY 10128
(212) 289-5514
Rep: Marlena Torzecka
(212) 289-5514

Sanders, Jane, 434
465 Lexington Ave. #33
New York, NY 10017
(212) 986-1827

Sano, Kazuhiko, 71, 72
105 Stadium Ave.
Mill Valley, CA 94941
(415) 381-6377

Scanlan, Michael, 311
27 Brookwood Dr.
Normal, IL 61761
(309) 452-6408

Schwartz, Daniel, 63, 332
48 E. 13th St. #8B
New York, NY 10003
(212) 533-0237
Rep: Richard Solomon
(212) 683-1362

INTERNATIONAL ARTIST INDEX

ART DIRECTORS, CLIENTS, AGENCIES

INTERNATIONAL ART DIRECTORS, CLIENTS, AGENCIES

PROFESSIONAL STATEMENTS

We Believe That Personal Vision Need Not Be the Exclusive Province of the Fine Artist

MASTER OF FINE ARTS IN ILLUSTRATION AS VISUAL ESSAY

This unique two year Master of Fine Arts program in Illustration is offered to commercial and fine artists who want to broaden their abilities to create personal statements in pictures and words. It is designed to encourage a personal, artistic vision through the development of the visual essay. It is an opportunity to learn how visual stories are developed and combined with text specifically for publication and gallery walls. To visit the *Master of Fine Arts in Illustration As Visual Essay Program* and discuss the program in detail, please call (212) 645-0458 for an appointment.

For further information call or write to the Office of Graduate Admissions.

FACULTY

MARSHALL ARISMAN
Chairman, Illustrator/Painter

GREGORY CRANE
Painter

PAUL DAVIS
Illustrator/Designer

LAURIE DOUGLAS
Computer Artist

CAROL FABRICATORE
Illustrator

MICHAEL FLANAGAN
Painter/Writer

STEVEN HELLER
Art Director

ELIZABETH HENLEY
Poet/Writer

CARL TITOLO
Painter

MARY JO VATH
Painter

THOMAS WOODRUFF
Illustrator/Painter

 School of VISUAL ARTS

A College of The Arts

209 East 23 Street, New York, NY 10010.   Tel 212.592.2100   Fax 212.592.2116

JOHN THOMPSON

206 Haddonfield Dr.

DeWitt, NY 13214

315.449.1241 tel

315.446.0241 fax

WORK BOOK

THINK PINK!

One wild shot could yank you right off the tree stand

from—*Why Nobody Hunts with a YOYO Anymore*

Dennis Dittrich 212-343-0096
395 Broadway Suite 10A New York N.Y. 10013

Talent

You've got it or you want to find it.

american **showcase** 2 1

also look for The Showcase CD.

915 Broadway 14th floor NYC 10010 (212) 673-6600 (800) 894-7469 info@amshow.com

The Norman Rockwell Museum

announces the first in a series of exclusive images,

created by Wendell Minor, illustrating four seasons

of the Museum's landscape. We are pleased to introduce you to

The Norman Rockwell Studio - Winter 1996

Prints and cards are now available at our Museum Store,

or you may order by phone: 1-800-742-9450

The Norman Rockwell Studio - Winter 1996, by Wendell Minor

The Norman Rockwell Museum *at Stockbridge, Massachusetts 01262*

DIRECTORY OF ILLUSTRATION

14

THANK YOU!

We are proud to announce that renewal advertising in the upcoming Graphic Artists Guild's *Directory of Illustration* has set an all-time record. This is our best indication of market satisfaction!

For more than 14 years, the *Directory of Illustration* has been generating business for commercial artists. We take this responsibility very seriously. The *Directory of Illustration* has a solid track record as an important link between the commercial illustrator and the creative buyer.

If your company is not receiving the *Directory of Illustration* and spends at least $50,000 per year on commercial illustration talent, you may qualify for a complimentary copy of this valuable source book. Please inquire for further information.

As an illustrator, advertising in the *Directory of Illustration* places your work among the best in the business. For more information on how the *Directory of Illustration* can help your business grow, please call for our 16 page brochure.

Directory of Illustration.
Published By Serbin Communications, Inc.
511 Olive Street
Santa Barbara, California 93101
Phone 800-876-6425
Fax   805-965-0496

FIRST CUPID
(CUPIDO PRIMUS)

THIS EARLY MESSENGER OF LOVE
WAS UNEARTHED IN PRISTINE CONDITION,
APRIL 18, 1908

O'BRIEN

Kirchoff/Wohlberg

Artists Representatives
866 United Nations Plaza
New York, NY 10017
(212) 644-2020

Tyrone Geter

Finally, illustrators can target the children's book market effectively.

Until now, getting your art seen by children's book publishers, art directors and editors has been a challenge. Postcards and mailers are filed or trashed and the larger art directories are not effective in this market. With *Picturebook*, the directory of children's book illustration, artists can get their work in front of top creative buyers and keep it there all year.

Picturebook was created by a children's book illustrator and the agent for the Margaret Wise Brown estate and it is changing the way artists and publishers communicate. To receive information on being included in *Picturebook 98*, or to order your own copy of *Picturebook 97*, call toll free: **888/490-0100** or fax: 205/595-0524

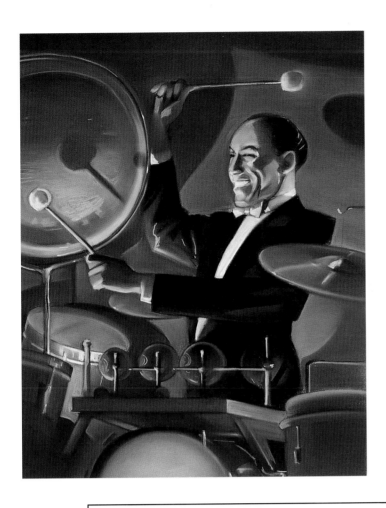

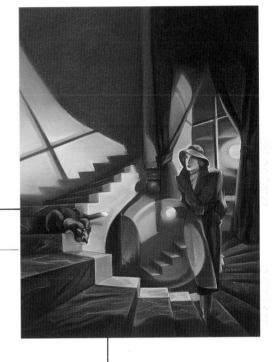

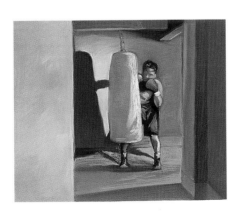

Great Illustrators Represent Gerald & Cullen Rapp

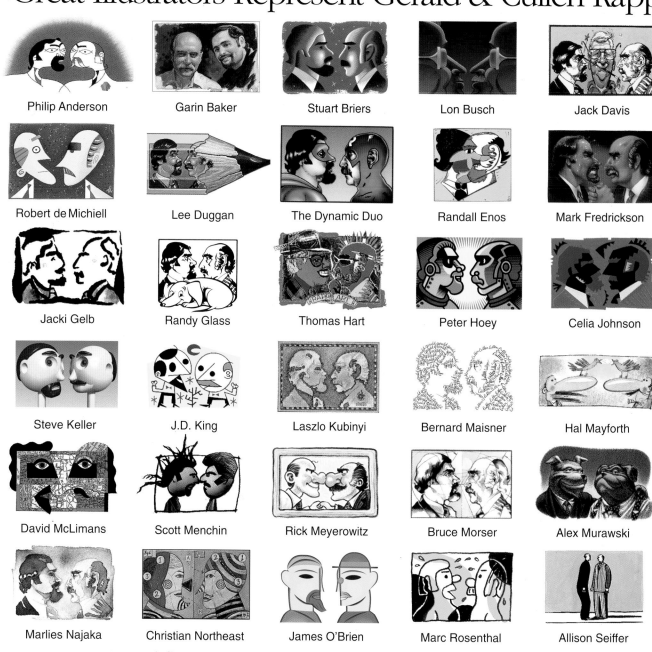

Philip Anderson	Garin Baker	Stuart Briers	Lon Busch	Jack Davis
Robert de Michiell	Lee Duggan	The Dynamic Duo	Randall Enos	Mark Fredrickson
Jacki Gelb	Randy Glass	Thomas Hart	Peter Hoey	Celia Johnson
Steve Keller	J.D. King	Laszlo Kubinyi	Bernard Maisner	Hal Mayforth
David McLimans	Scott Menchin	Rick Meyerowitz	Bruce Morser	Alex Murawski
Marlies Najaka	Christian Northeast	James O'Brien	Marc Rosenthal	Allison Seiffer
Mark Stearney	James Steinberg	Drew S.	Michael Witte	Bob Ziering

Gerald & Cullen Rapp
Has Represented Great Illustrators Since 1944

Ask first.

Copyright
Clearance Center

Advertising Photographers
of America

Advertising Photographers
of New York

Society of
Illustrators

June, 1996

Dear Colleague:

As partners in the creative process, the organizations listed below are joining with *Copyright Clearance Center* in sponsoring this copyright awareness campaign. We encourage you to respect private intellectual property and the copyright laws that govern it.

Art or photography in portfolios submitted for a job should not be copied for any use, including client presentation or "comping," without the creator's permission. Similarly, images appearing in any of the talent sourcebooks and directories (either in print or electronically), should not be "swiped" for any reason. In case after case, the creator's property rights have been upheld, and those caught engaging in these practices were penalized, paying large fines to the artists.

We appreciate your desire to use our images. Even more, we are flattered and complimented. But for a number of reasons, artists may not want to have their images used in any way, including agency representations. And any use, including "comping," implies value that is worth some compensation.

Please, call before copying.

S P A R
Society of Photographers and
Artists Representatives

Society of Publication
Designers

American Society of
Media Photographers

chicago
artist
representatives

Type Directors Club

THE
**BLACK
BOOK**

PHOTO DISTRICT NEWS

RSVP
THE DIRECTORY
OF ILLUSTRATION
& DESIGN

SERBIN
COMMUNICATIONS

WORK
BOOK

Mark design by the Pushpin Group

SOCIETY ACTIVITIES

STEVAN DOHANOS AWARD Rafal Olbinski

OUR OWN SHOW
1996

THE SOCIETY OF ILLUSTRATORS
MEMBERS SEVENTH ANNUAL
OPEN EXHIBITION

*"Our Own Show" is pleased to inaugurate the
Stevan Dohanos Award as the Best in Show
in this open, unjuried exhibition.*

AWARD OF MERIT Thomas B. Allen

Society of Illustrators

"Our Own Show" was created to extend this annual opportunity for all professionally active members of the Society to exhibit a work in the Museum galleries. Each year nearly 200 artists participate.

"Our Own Show" is the major funding source for the Ten Year Rebuilding plan which is modernizing the Society's 1875 Carriage House headquarters for the 21st Century.

AWARD OF MERIT Shinichiro Tora

No secret handshake
No dress code
No dangerous initiation rites

C.F. PAYNE

Now's a good time to join

Isn't it about time you made some artist
friends to talk to? The Society of Illustrators is
now accepting applications in the following
membership categories: Artist; Associate;
Corporate; Educator; Student and Friend of
the Museum. For details, call or write the Society
and ask for a membership packet.

 Society of Illustrators

128 East 63rd Street
New York, N.Y. 10021
212-838-2560

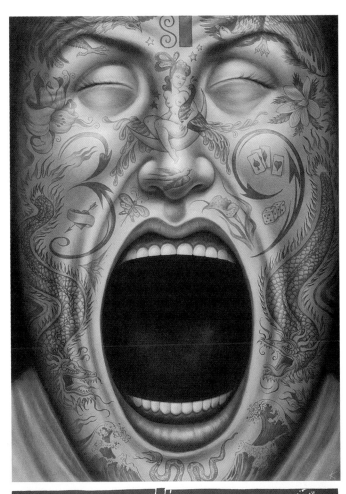

INTERNATIONAL
CATEGORY

DEADLINE: FEBRUARY 14, 1997

Illustration by Anita Kunz • Type Design by D.J. Stout

SOCIETY OF ILLUSTRATORS • 128 EAST 63RD STREET • NEW YORK, NY 10021 • USA • FAX 011-212-838-2561

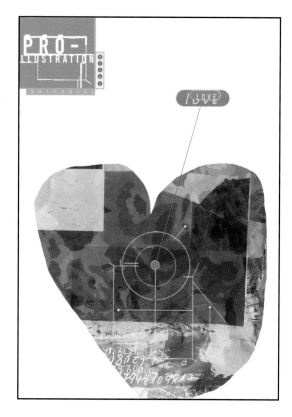

PRO-ILLUSTRATION
Volume One
EDITORIAL ILLUSTRATION

by Jill Bossert
A Guide to Professional Illustration
Techniques
Sponsored by the Society of Illustrators

Guy Billout

The first in the **PRO-ILLUSTRATION** series, this full-color book gives a professional look at award-winning illustration techniques. It's a unique opportunity to see how nine of the Society's top illustrators tackle an editorial project from assignment to finished artwork.

Joan Hall

The Society of Illustrators has simulated an editorial assignment for a Sunday magazine supplement surveying the topic of "Love." Topics assigned to the illustrators include: Erotic Love, First Love, Weddings, Sensual Love, Computer Love, Adultery and Divorce. The stages of execution from, initial sketch to finish, are shown in a series of photographs and accompanying text. It's a unique, behind-the-scenes look at each illustrator's studio and the secrets of their individual styles. Professional techniques demonstrated include oil, acrylic, collage, computer, etching, trompe l' oeil, dyes and airbrush.

Barbara Nessim

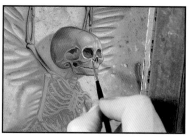

Tim O'Brien

In addition to the demonstrations, each illustrator has a portfolio section, showing his or her best work. This book is a must for all aspiring professional illustrators.

Size: 8 5/8 x 11 3/4 • Pages: 160
Designed by Eric Baker Design
Published by RotoVision S.A.
ISBN 0-8230-6549

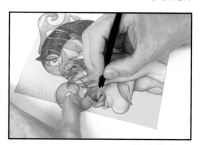

Mel Odom

THE ARTISTS ARE:

Marshall Arisman
Guy Billout
Alan E. Cober
Elaine Duillo
Joan Hall
Wilson McLean
Barbara Nessim
Tim O'Brien
Mel Odom

Please send _____ copies of **PRO-ILLUSTRATION**, Volume One at $29.95 plus $4.00 per copy for postage. Postage to Canada is $9.00. Overseas is $15.00 (New York residents add $2.47 sales tax.)

MAIL TO: Society of Illustrators, 128 East 63rd Street, New York, NY 10021-7303

Make check payable to the Society of Illustrators, in United States funds drawn on a United States bank.

Charge my credit card: American Express ❑   Visa ❑   Master Card ❑

Account number: _____ Expiration date: _____/_____

Signature: _____

Print Name: _____

You may FAX your credit card order to: (212) 838-2561. Please allow 4 weeks for delivery.

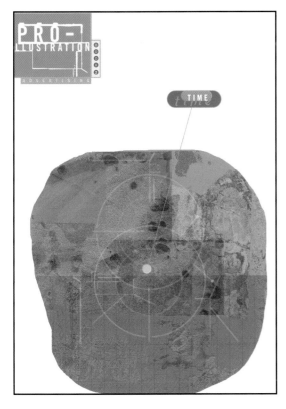

PRO-ILLUSTRATION
Volume Two

ADVERTISING ILLUSTRATION
by Jill Bossert
A Guide to Professional Illustration Techniques
Sponsored by the Society of Illustrators

N. Ascencios

The second in the **PRO-ILLUSTRATION** series, this full-color book gives a professional look at award-winning illustration techniques. It's a singular opportunity to see how nine of America's top illustrators tackle an advertising project from assignment to finished artwork.

Robert M. Cunningham

The Society of Illustrators has simulated an advertising campaign for a fictitious manufacturer of timepieces. The overall concept is "Time" and nine of the very best illustrators put their talents to solving the problem. The stages of execution, from initial phone call to finish, are described in photographs and text. You'll understand the demonstration of the techniques used to create a final piece of art. It's a unique behind-the-scenes look at each illustrator's studio and the secrets of their individual styles. Professional techniques demonstrated include oil, acrylic, mixed media collage, computer, three-dimension and airbrush.

Mark Hess

THE ARTISTS ARE:

N. Ascencios
Mark Borow
Robert M. Cunningham
Teresa Fasolino
Mark Hess
Hiro Kimura
Rafal Olbinski
Fred Otnes
Chris Spollen

Fred Otnes

In addition to the demonstrations, a portfolio section shows each illustrator's most exciting work. This book is a must for all aspiring and professional illustrators, instructors and illustration buyers.

Size: 8 5/8 x 11 3/4 • Pages: 160
Designed by Eric Baker Design
Published by RotoVision S.A.

Chris Spollen

Please send _____ copies of **PRO-ILLUSTRATION**, Volume Two at $29.95 plus $4.00 per copy for postage. Postage to Canada is $9.00. Overseas is $15.00 (New York residents add $2.47 sales tax.)

MAIL TO: Society of Illustrators, 128 East 63rd Street, New York, NY 10021-7303

Make check payable to the Society of Illustrators, in United States funds drawn on a United States bank.

Charge my credit card: American Express ❑   Visa ❑   Master Card ❑

Account number: _____ Expiration date: _____/_____

Signature: _____

Print Name: _____

You may FAX your credit card order to: (212) 838-2561. Please allow 4 weeks for delivery.

Through the generous support of Mobil Foundation, Inc., the Society has been able to bring nationally recognized illustrators to New York for "An Evening With...." These informative, yet informal presentations in the casual, yet historical setting of the Society's Members Dining Room, have been videotaped and made available to college-level art programs nationwide.

What began in the 1930's as panel discussions to local artists by such luminaries as Norman Rockwell, James Montgomery Flagg and Charles Dana Gibson, are now a national forum for today's top illustrators.

The Society expresses its deep appreciation to
the MOBIL FOUNDATION for its seven consecutive years of support.
Through them we have gone NATIONAL.

Spring **1996** *Lecture Series*

April 24

Panel Discussion on Computers

John Ennis
Barbara Nessim
Chris Spollen

May 1

**Self Publishing –
Limited Edition Prints**

Bill Harbort
Chuck Movicker
Murray Tinkelman
Moderator

May 8

"An Evening With . . ."
James Gurney

Paul Davis

James Gurney

fall **1996** *Lecture Series*

Nov 6

**"Selling Rights—
The Second Time Around"**

Karen D'Silva
The Image Bank
M.C. Matter
Stock Illustration Source
Daniel Pelavin

Nov 13

"The Artist as Journalist"

Gil Cohen
Christine Cornell
Dick Rockwell
Carol Fabricatore

Dec 4

"An Evening with Paul Davis"

For information regarding videotapes of these presentations, for educational use. Call 1-800-SIMUSEUM

society of illustrators
digital show
1996

The Society's first ever look at the latest in commercial applications of computer art is reproduced in this 32 page catalogue - in full color. $10.00 plus $3.00 postage.

A special limited edition (350) print of this image by Steve Lyons. $10.00 (Shipping and handling add $3.00), 15" x 27", 5 colors on heavy archival stock.

SOUNDS FROM THE BULLPEN

BY HOWARD MUNCE

A collection of bleats, bitches & bellyaches anent the calamities & vicissitudes of the minority known as commercial artists.

A collection of outrageous satirical essays about the working life of commercial artists of every stripe. This 80 page, black & white, hard-cover book deals with artists in commerce as they naively tilt at enemy windmills that stretch to the horizon.

This collection was originally written for Bulletin Editor Arpi Ermoyan, for the entertainment and enlightenment of members of the Society of Illustrators and appeared infrequently in the Society's newsletter.

Munce & Webster define "BULL-PEN n.

ART as an enclosure where a collection ofcommercial artists of diverse specialities are corralled like bulls and prisoners in remote and windowless sections of office buildings to keep *t*hem from rioting. They are kept warmed-up until burnt-out in a game that deals only in emergencies and never progresses. Their seats at their drawing boards become lifelong penalty benches." Munce adds "if this volume has nothing else to recommend it, you will find it just thick enough to stabilize a short-legged table or to urge parents of young people of art school age to sell them to gyp-sies, enlist them in the Foreign Legion or

fast-freeze them until computer graphics take over."

Author Howard Munce is a scarred veteran of 16 years in 6 New York advertising agencies and 30 plus years as a freelance art director, illustrator, and all-around hand and head for hire.

This uniquely, madly written book is for everyone from art student to professional graphics practitioner. It's aimed at all ranks--and all senses of humor. And it is profusely illustrated by the author.

Please send_____ copies of SOUNDS FROM THE BULLPEN at $25.00 plus $5.00 per copy for postage and handling in the United States. Postage and handling to Canada is $9.00, overseas is $15.00. (New York residents add 8 1/4% sales tax.)

MAIL TO: Society of Illustrators, 128 East 63rd Street, New York, NY 10021-7303

Make checks payable to the Society of Illustrators, in United States funds drawn on a United States bank.

Charge my credit card: American Express ❏   Visa ❏   Master Card ❏

Account number: _____ Expiration date:_____

Signature: _____

Print Name: _____

City:_____ State: _____ Zip:_____

You may FAX your credit card order to: (212) 838-2561. Please allow 4 weeks for delivery.

The ILLUSTRATOR IN AMERICA 1880·1980

By Walt & Roger Reed

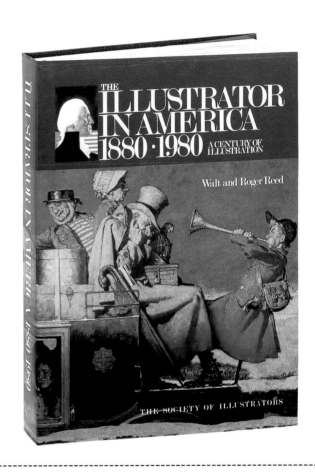

This major reference work of the history of modern illustration includes all the important illustrators, and representations of their work, of the late 19th and 20th centuries. This volume acts as a complete course of this period of American illustration and for this reason is a most valued tool for understanding the history of illustration in this period.

•••

Walt and Roger Reed, respected historians of American illustration, have done a masterful job of selecting the most appropriate images to represent each of the 460 illustrators in this book.

The artists appear in the decade in which their influence was most strongly felt.

Each decade is introduced by a famous illustrator with comprehensive knowledge of the period. Included is a biographical sketch of each of the 460 artists, setting forth all the facts needed to help in the understanding of the artists and their work.

This lavishly produced 9" X 12" 352 page book, containing 700 illustrations, many in full color, by 460 artists is a must for the serious student or collector and a valuable reference for everyone in the profession.

Please send _____ copies of ILLUSTRATOR IN AMERICA 1880/1980 at $48.50 plus $5.00 per copy for postage and handling in the United States. Postage and handling to Canada is $9.00, overseas is $15.00. (New York residents add 8 1/4% sales tax.)

MAIL TO: Society of Illustrators, 128 East 63rd Street, New York, NY 10021-7303

Make checks payable to the Society of Illustrators, in United States funds drawn on a United States bank.

Charge my credit card: American Express ❏   Visa ❏   Master Card ❏

Account number: _____   Expiration date: _____

Signature: _____

Print Name: _____

You may FAX your credit card order to: (212) 838-2561. Please allow 4 weeks for delivery.

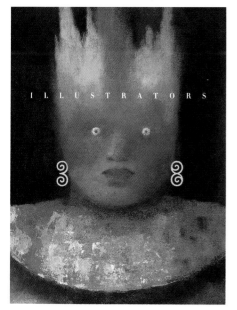

Society of Illustrators

Museum Shop

The Society of Illustrators Museum of American Illustration maintains a shop featuring many quality products. Four-color, large format books document contemporary illustration and the great artists of the past. Museum quality prints and posters capture classic images. T-shirts, sweatshirts, hats, mugs and tote bags make practical and fun gifts.

The Museum Shop is an extension of the Society's role as the center for illustration in America today. For further information or quantity discounts, contact the Society at TEL: (212) 838-2560 / FAX: (212) 838-2561

NEW!
ILLUSTRATORS 38
352 pp. Cover by Brad Holland. Contains the 452 works accepted by the juries. Also the 56 works accepted in the International Category. Hall of Fame, Hamilton King Awards.The most contemporary look at Illustration world wide.
$59.50

ILLUSTRATORS ANNUAL BOOKS

These catalogs are based on our annual juried exhibitions, divided into four major categories in American Illustration: Editorial, Book, Advertising, and Institutional. Some are available in a limited supply only.

In addition, a limited number of out-of-print collector's editions of the Illustrators Annuals that are not listed above (1959 to Illustrators 30) are available as is.

Also available for collectors are back issues of The Art Directors Club annuals and GRAPHIS Annuals.

Contact the Society for details...

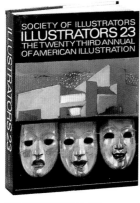

ILLUSTRATORS 23
$20.00
limited number remaining

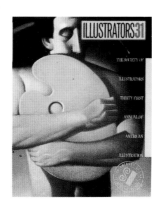

ILLUSTRATORS 31
$25.00

ILLUSTRATORS 32
$25.00
limited number remaining

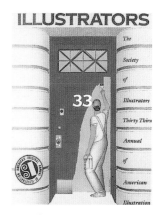

ILLUSTRATORS 33
$25.00

ILLUSTRATORS 34
$40.00

ILLUSTRATORS 36
$45.00

ILLUSTRATORS 37
$49.95

ART FOR SURVIVAL
$25.00

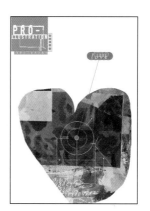

PRO-ILLUSTRATION
Volume One - Editorial
160 pp, full color book gives a professional look at award-winning illustration techniques. $29.95

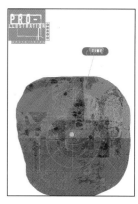

PRO-ILLUSTRATION
Volume Two - Advertising
160 pp, full color book gives a professional look at award-winning illustration techniques. $29.95

SOCIETY OF ILLUSTRATORS • 128 East 63rd Street • New York, NY 10021

Dean Cornwell, "Gold Hands", Cosmopolitan, 1923
$12.00

Mead Schaeffer, "Stagecoach Holdup" The American Magazine, 1937
$12.00

Joseph Christian Leyendecker,"Easter" The Saturday
Evening Post, 1935 © Curtis Publishing 1935 $12.00

N.C. Wyeth,"The Black Arrow" by Robert Louis
Stevenson Charles Scribner's Sons, 1916 $12.00

MUSEUM QUALITY POSTERS

**Posters of classic works from the Society's Permanent Collection.
Reproduced on glossy stock in a 11"x15" format.
Suitable for framing. $12.00 per poster; $38.00 for the set of four.**

EXHIBITION POSTERS

**Posters created for exhibitions in the Society of Illustrators Museum of American
Illustration. Suitable for framing. $10.00 per poster; $27.00 for the set of three.**

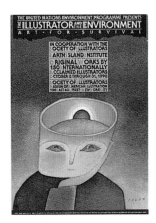

**"Recycled Ideas"
"The Illustrator and the
Environment "
by FOLON $10.00**

"Science Fiction" by JOHN BERKEY, 1984
$10.00

"Wizard of Oz", The Original Art by EDWARD SOREL, 1991
$10.00

UNIQUE EDITION

150 pages in full color of Children's books from 1992. This volume contains valuable "how-to" comments from the artists as well as a publishers directory. A compilation of the exhibition, "The Original Art 1992 - Celebrating the Fine Art of Children's Book Illustration."
$29.95

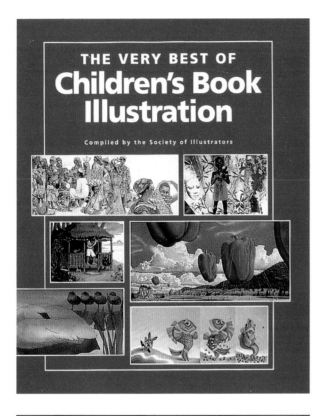

NEW ITEMS

11oz. ceramic mugs featuring works from the Society of Illustrators Permanent Collection. Artist: John Held Jr., Norman Rockwell and J.C. Leyendecker. Set of 3 only $20.00.

THE BUSINESS LIBRARY

Each of thesee volumes is a valuable asset to the professional artist whether established or just starting out. Together they form a solid base for your business.

The set of three volumes. $42.00

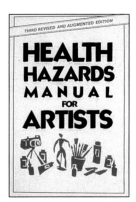

GRAPHIC ARTISTS GUILD HANDBOOK PRICING AND ETHICAL GUIDELINES - Vol. 7
Includes an outline of ethical standards and business practices, as well as price ranges for hundreds of uses and sample contracts.
$22.95

THE LEGAL GUIDE FOR THE VISUAL ARTIST
1994 Edition.
Tad Crawford's text explains basic copyrights, moral rights, the sale of rights, taxation, business accounting and the legal support groups available to artists.
$18.95

HEALTH HAZARDS MANUAL
A comprehensive review of materials and supplies, from fixatives to pigments, airbrushes to solvents.
$9.95

GIFT ITEMS

The Society's famous Red and Black logo, designed by Bradbury Thompson, is featured on the following gift items:

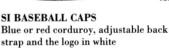

SI LAPEL PINS
$6.00
Actual Size

SI BASEBALL CAPS
Blue or red corduroy, adjustable back strap and the logo in white
$15.00

SI TOTE BAGS
Heavyweight, white canvas bags are 14" high with the two-color logo
$15.00

SI PATCH
White with blue lettering and piping - 4" wide
$4.00

SI CERAMIC COFFEE MUGS
Heavyweight 14 oz. mugs are white with the two-color logo
$6.00 each, $20.00 for a set of 4

SI T-SHIRTS

Incorporating the Soicety's 1962 logo by Bradbury Thompson. White, heavy cotton shirt with two-color logo. $10.00 each. Sizes: Small, Large, X-Large, XX-Large.

38th Annual Exhibition • Frog to Prince by Jack Unruh • 100% cotton pocket T $15.00. Large, X-Large, XX-Large

SI SWEATSHIRTS

Blue with white lettering of multiple logos. Grey with large red SI. $20.00 each. Sizes: Large, X-Large, XX-Large.

SI NOTE CARDS

Norman Rockwell greeting cards, 3-7/8" x 8-5/8", inside blank, great for all occasions. Includes 100% rag envelopes

10 cards - $10.00
20 cards - $18.00
50 cards - $35.00
100 cards - $60.00

ORDER FORM

Mail to the attention of:
The Museum Shop, SOCIETY OF ILLUSTRATORS, 128 East 63rd Street, New York, NY 10021   38

NAME _____

COMPANY_____

STREET_____

CITY_____

STATE_____ZIP _____

DAYTIME PHONE (___) _____

Enclosed is my check for $ _____
Make checks payable to Society of Illustrators
Please charge my credit card:

❏ American Express   ❏ Master Card   ❏ Visa

Card Number _____

Signature _____ Expiration Date _____

*please note if name appearing on the card is different than the mailing name.

Qty	Description	Size	Color	Price	Total
# of items ordered			Total price of item(s) ordered		
			*Shipping/handling per order		4.00
			TOTAL DUE		

* Foreign postage additional

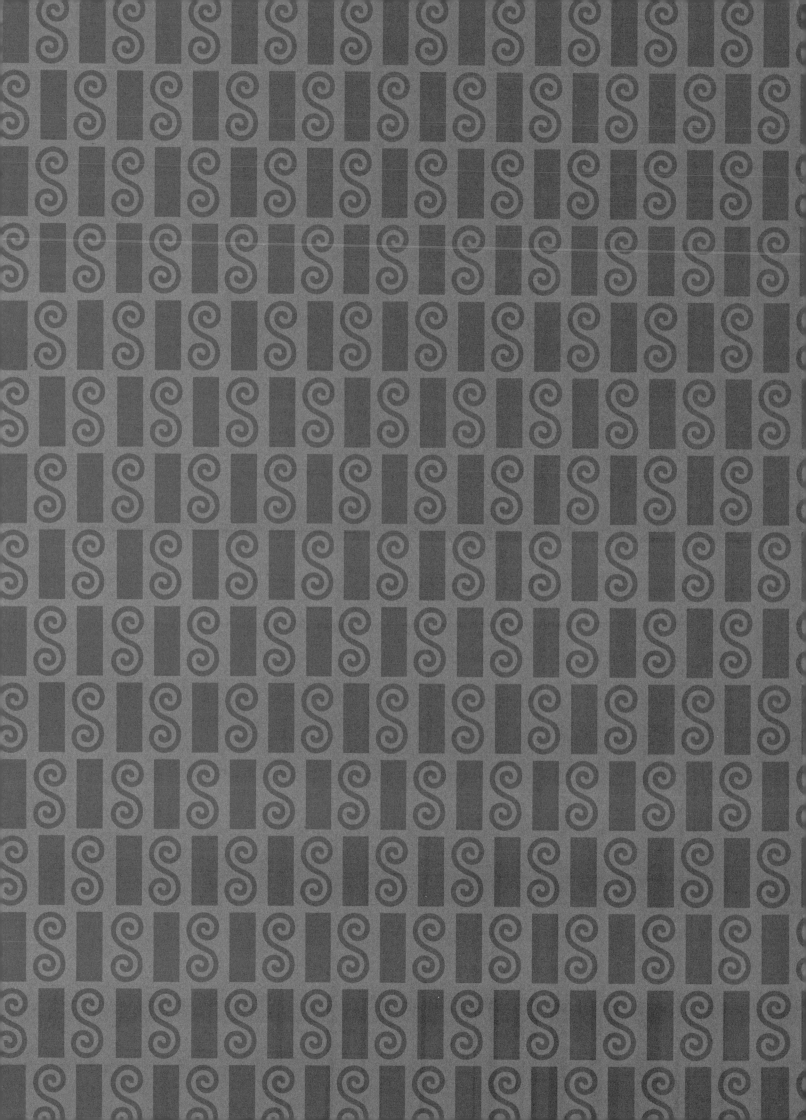